AIRFIX ANNUAL
for
MILITARY MODELLERS

Edited by Bruce Quarrie

Patrick Stephens Ltd, Cambridge
in association with
Airfix Products Ltd, London

First published — 1978

British Library Cataloguing in Publication Data
Airfix annual for military modellers.
  1. Military miniatures 2. Models and
  model making 3. Plastics craft
  I. Quarrie, Bruce
  745.59'282   NK8475.M5

ISBN 0 85059 314 X

Text set in 9 on 10 Helvetica Medium by
Blackfriars Press Limited, Leicester. Printed in
Great Britain on 100 gsm Pedigree Cartridge
and bound by The Garden City Press, Letchworth
for the publishers Patrick Stephens Limited,
Bar Hill, Cambridge, CB3 8EL, in association
with Airfix Products Limited, London SW18.

Editor's introduction

A warm welcome to the first *Airfix Annual for Military Modellers*. This exciting new book has been produced in response to requests from readers of the previous *Airfix Magazine Annuals* for more specialised treatment of their own subjects which would make the book more relevant for them, and you can judge the result for yourself.

The increasing trend amongst modellers seems to be towards greater and deeper specialisation in one subject or group of related subjects, and this Annual has been designed to meet the requirements of those who build military vehicles, figures, guns or ships. A separate volume is available for any of your friends who specialise in model aircraft.

This book includes ideas for converting and scratch-building as well as plans and photographs for other subjects which lend themselves to re-creation in miniature, such as the Soviet heavy tanks at Leningrad or Hungarian artillery pieces; both of which are neglected subjects which could be turned into attractive model collections with the use of a little imagination, the accompanying illustrations, parts of Airfix and other plastic kits, and oddments of plastic card, rod, sprue, etc. Other subjects are described in more detail for those readers less experienced in working on their own — such as Jeremy Broughton's Conqueror tank conversion,

Gerald Scarborough's Mack truck or John Sandars' Bofors gun; Rob Gibson's simple figure conversions, Roy Dilley's gun detachment (which shows how plastic and metal models can be combined to make a very attractive diorama), or Ian Fleming's HMS *Renown*.

An interest in military modelling often leads directly into wargaming, and *vice versa,* so there are also some ideas in this field, ranging from three Napoleonic subjects to armoured warfare in the Far East (another grossly neglected subject) and simple Airfix Forward Command Post conversions.

So there is ample material here for virtually every military modeller, but remember that the Airfix model range is constantly expanding and that similar ideas and subjects are covered every month in *Airfix Magazine*. Above all, good modelling depends on the exercise of the imagination even more than development of individual skills, and even a model which does not appeal to you may spark off an idea for a similar treatment in a different field. So don't just read the things which interest you — read everything you can, whether it appears relevant or not. Above all, hoard photographs and drawings like a miser. That way, you'll never be short of inspiration.

Bruce Quarrie

Contents

CONQUEROR!

Jeremy Broughton shows how to model this formidable British heavy tank in 1:76 scale

The heaviest tank to see service since World War 2 has been the British Conqueror Heavy Gun Tank, and indeed it seems unlikely that its combat weight of 65 tons will be exceeded in the future. The Conqueror was introduced in limited numbers in 1955, and was intended to support the more lightly armed Centurion tanks; to this end it was equipped with the prominent 120 mm gun and elaborate fire control devices in order to destroy heavy enemy tanks at long ranges. This led to very heavy armour protection, and the vehicle's high weight tended to reduce manoeuvrability. The introduction of Centurions armed with the 105 mm gun led to the withdrawal of the Conqueror in the mid-1960s, after a relatively short period of service. Nonetheless, it is a very impressive tank to see and an interesting subject for a model.

The model that I shall describe and the accompanying plans are to 1:76 scale. Some parts from the Airfix Centurion tank kit will be needed, but the model is largely scratch-built from sheet plastic of various thicknesses. The most convenient place to begin is the hull top. The well within which the turret is to be placed must be formed first, so mark out on a sheet of 40 thou plastic card a rectangle 66 mm by 27 mm and locate the turret centre point 28 mm from the leading edge and midway between the longer sides. Using dividers, scribe a circle of radius 12½ mm and a second circle of radius 17½ mm, then carefully cut around the inner circle and remove the disc which will be used later as the base of the turret. Mark a line parallel to and 17 mm behind the leading edge of the rectangle. You have now drawn a rectangle with lobes projecting on

---

Title photo *Conqueror splashing through a pool of mud on manoeuvres.* **Below** *Front three-quarter view of finished model.* **Below right** *Rear view.*

either side of the turret well; cut this out and divide it into two along the latest line.

The hull sides are made next. Start by drawing them full size on a sheet of 20 thou plastic, then take 1 mm from the forward inclined edges to allow for the overlap of the plates that will fit over them. A 1 mm deep recess is needed on the upper edge to accept the lobe on the upper plate. Cut out the plates, and file a 45 degrees bevel on the upper edge of each, forward of the recess. To ensure a square assembly of the side and top plates, use rectangular bulkheads mounted below each part of the top plate. Cement the plates together, and while the cement hardens cut the remaining faces of the hull from 40 thou sheet, remembering that the two forward faces are 1 mm wider than the others. Then cement them in place in sequence, starting at the rear part of the hull top and working around to the glacis plate.

The engine covers can now be detailed. The louvres are the trickiest parts, and there are three sets, 5 mm, 7 mm and 8 mm deep respectively. To make a particular set take a 20 thou rectangle of the appropriate width and approximately 40 mm long then, using a steel ruler as a guide, score a series of parallel lines along the rectangle. This is achieved with the point of a sharp knife, held vertically with the blunt edge of the blade held against the ruler, drawn along two or three times to leave a fine triangular groove ½ mm wide. With practice a uniform effect can be obtained. Trim either end to leave a 27 mm length.

Before the louvres are cemented to the hull top attach a 27 mm by 3 mm rectangle of 40 thou sheet across the top plate, which will later carry the engine cover mountings; the two wider sets of louvres fit on either side of this strip. In front of the forward set cement a 27 mm by 9 mm rectangle of 10 thou sheet, and the narrowest set of louvres fits in front of this. Another 10 thou rectangle should be positioned between the rear louvres and the uppermost part of the rear plate.

The Conqueror's engine covers actually comprise seven pairs of panels, each panel being supported by large hinges on a central bar. The panel details and hinges can all be reproduced from plastic strip.

The trackguards and suspension are now added to the basic hull. This work is greatly simplified by the fact that the extensive side-shields carried by all Conquerors conceal all of the suspension units and half of the track. Each trackguard should be supported by a pair of brackets which can be shaped to carry the side-shields when they are added later: this is shown in the cross-section drawing. 32 road wheels are now needed, and they can be conveniently made from plastic sheet. Cut out a series of 7 mm squares from strips of 40 thou sheet, then trim each square to a rough disc and use a file for the final shaping. When you have 32 reasonably circular discs, make another 32 discs, of 3 mm diameter, from 20 thou strips, then cement each of the smaller discs to the centre of one of the larger discs. Now choose the 16 better wheels — these will become the visible road wheels — and cement the 'axle' of each of the poorer wheels to the inner face of one of the better wheels. As the suspension units will be invisible they can be represented very simply by 40 thou rectangles attached to the hull side with brackets, and each double wheel is cemented directly to one of these rectangles. As you mount the wheels take care that they are accurately aligned, so that when the model is placed on a flat surface the hull does not rock and all wheels are in contact with the surface.

I used the sprocket and idler wheels from a Centurion kit in the model illustrated and, although slightly undersize, they achieve the right effect. I cut the corresponding axles, complete with the supporting plastic, from the Centurion hull side plates and filed the inner faces down in order that when the units were cemented to the hull sides the axles were horizontal.

The production of the track from plastic sheet is, admittedly, a tedious job but much of the outer surface is hidden so that only limited detailing is needed. Before the track is cemented in place a certain amount of painting is required, including

Side view of finished model.

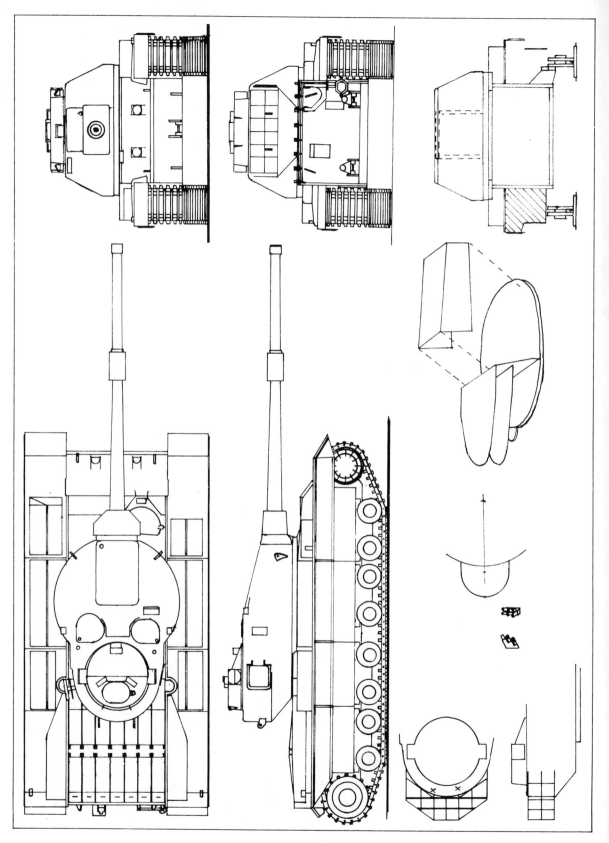

the tracks — a metallic grey — and the wheels. The Conqueror road wheels are of an unusual pattern, with a rubber tyre enclosed by a steel tyre, so that the outer faces of the wheels are painted green and the wheel rim a steel colour. When the tracks are in place the sets of side-shields are cut from 10 thou sheet and mounted on the trackguard brackets.

The main part of the construction of the hull is now complete and a range of details will be added later. For the moment however we will turn to the turret.

Begin by cutting out two discs: the first of 35 mm diameter from 60 thou sheet and the second of 35½ mm diameter from 40 thou sheet. Cement them together so that the upper overlaps the lower evenly, then cement the 25 mm disc cut earlier from the hull top plate centrally to the lower disc. This unit forms the turret base which fits into the turret well in the hull; check that it will rotate freely within the well.

The Conqueror turret consists largely of a massive steel casting, and to reproduce this we will use a combination of two methods. Where the turret surface is flat or curved in one plane only, plastic sheet is attached to a strong internal skeleton, but where the shape is more complex — as for example on either side of the gun mantlet — putty is used. It would be possible, instead of using putty, to build up these shapes by cementing together layers of thick plastic and you may find this easier. I have included a sketch of the way in which the turret skeleton is built up, but for some pieces allowance must be made when measuring from the plans for the thickness of the pieces that will fit over the skeleton.

Towards the rear the turret has a flat roof upon which the independent 'Fire Control Turret' is carried. This roof is an elongated D-shape, which extends forward as far as the rear face of the gunner's sight to the right of the turret axis. The sides beside the pair of hatches are parallel, and 26 mm apart. Mark this out full size on a 40 thou sheet of plastic, then remove ½ mm from all edges but the front and cut the roof out to this inner profile. Next cut out a second identical piece and trim 1 mm from its front edge, then file a 45 degrees bevel on

the lower half of the outer edge. Cement two 6 mm wide strips in a 'T' on top of the second piece, then fit the roof on the upper edges of the 'T' taking great care over the alignment.

The floor of the turret bustle is an extension of the upper disc of the turret base assembly. Take a sheet of 40 thou plastic and mark two points 19 mm apart. Draw circles of radius 6½ mm and 18 mm with these two centres, then draw parallel tangents from the smaller circle to intersect the larger; this is illustrated in one of the plans. Cut out this shape, cement the larger arc to the circumference of the turret base and file a 45 degrees bevel to the outer edge.

The next piece needed is the bulkhead that will carry the roof. Cut out a rectangle 12 mm by 34 mm, then cut away triangles 4 mm by 9 mm from the upper corners and cement it on the turret base at 90 degrees to the turret axis and 4 mm behind the centre. The roof assembly is added to the bulkhead rear, with the roof overlapping the bulkhead. Next the inclined lower face of the bustle is built up by cementing first one and then a second strip of 10 thou sheet around the skeleton, extending only as far forward as the turret base. When this has thoroughly set trim the rough edges, the lower being flush with the bustle floor and the upper being slightly below the upper face of the horizontal support. The upper, vertical, face of the bustle is then built up in the same way, with the 10 thou strips fitting into the step just formed. The skeleton for the forward part of the turret is added next. This is a simple box, the upper face being a rectangle 20 mm by 13 mm and the forward face 6½ mm by 13 mm.

Putty is now used to build up the remaining surfaces. These comprise two large bulbous areas on either side of the gun mounting and two smaller areas behind the bulkhead adjoining the bustle. When the putty has set really hard begin by shaving away the excess with a sharp knife and then, when

Notes on the plans

The plans are to 1:76 scale and show a Conqueror Mark 2 Heavy Gun Tank. The smoke discharger unit, turret stowage rack and bottom of the turret bustle are drawn separately, to scale. There is also a cross-section of the model taken at the main turret bulkhead just behind the gunner's periscope; broken lines show the position of the forward parts of the turret skeleton, the shaded part to the left of the hull shows the trackguard support and to the right the simplified suspension mounting is seen. The perspective sketch, not to scale, depicts the main parts of the turret skeleton.

Turret removed to show underside detail.

Above *Interesting shot of a Conqueror Mk II in Germany, probably in 1961. It carries the crossed key and bayonet on red background surmounted by a blue '5' of the 5th Infantry Brigade and an unidentified arm of service badge on the hull front, plus a yellow bridging disc with black '80' on the mudguard, while the crew members wear black berets with RTR badge. Can anyone identify the precise unit and location?* **Below** *Early Conqueror being put through its places at the Fighting Vehicle Research and Development Establishment (FVRDE) at Chobham, Surrey. Alongside is a 20 pdr-armed Centurion.*

the required form is almost achieved, use a file for the final shaping. Proceed cautiously: if too much putty is removed it is difficult to bond a small additional blob to the main mass. With the final shaping of the putty goes the rounding of the bustle edges, and when this has been completed apply a coat of white paint to show up any slight defects and to give a uniform base for the final painting.

The gun barrel is produced next, using the thickest piece of circular sprue that you possess. If, as is quite likely, this is not sufficiently thick, build up one end with spiral strips of 10 thou plastic. In the first stage of shaping a folded piece of sandpaper is most useful, but a file is needed for the final smoothing. When the barrel is ready add the fume extractor from layers of 10 thou sheet, then build up a mantlet from 40 thou plastic, cement the barrel in place and mount the assembly on the vertical forward face of the turret. A flexible dust cover hides the gap between the mantlet and the turret, and this is reproduced from strips of tissue paper.

The secondary turret is now built up in much the same way. Cut out the base and two-piece roof and cement them to an internal skeleton, then cement a curved 10 thou strip around the outer edges. When this has set trim away the excess plastic, then build up the small extensions on either side: these represent armoured covers for either end of the commander's rangefinder, and on the front of each is a protective flap. Now add the commander's hatch, periscopes and the various other details before fitting the turret on to the roof of the main turret. The hatches, hooks etc of the main turret can then be added from plastic sheet, and the cable reel from a Centurion kit is mounted on the left of the bustle. A smoke discharger unit is mounted on either side of the turret which, because of the turret form, is carried at a slope. For clarity I have drawn a unit separately, and have shown the mountings in position on the turret. The body of each unit can be made up from three sloping pieces of 40 thou sheet, one for each pair of barrels, and the barrels then added from stubs of stretched sprue. The only feature now remaining is the stowage rack carried on the turret rear, which is reproduced from stretched sprue. The sprue should be of approximately ¼ mm diameter, and it is important to use only those lengths that are straight and of constant thickness. The easiest approach is to begin with the lower outer rail and, laying the assembly on the drawing, add the various inner rails. When this is complete add the vertical bars and then fit the upper rail. The middle rail is cemented along the inside of the bars; cement is then applied to the ends of the three horizontal rails and the rack is fixed to the turret rear. There are two more points of attachment; cement short lengths of sprue beneath the inner ends of the rails at the points marked 'X' on the plan, and attach them to the turret.

Now that the turret is complete a certain amount of work remains on the hull. The first job is the completion of the turret ring, for there will be a gap bet-

Rear view of a Conqueror Mk II with camouflage netting strapped to the turret rear.

ween the turret base and the sloping plate behind the glacis. Cut from 20 thou sheet a 'D' shape of 18 mm radius and 6 mm depth and cement it to the sloping plate. When the cement is set trim away the portion obstructing the turret well, then file the upper face flush with the horizontal hull top. Make sure that this piece now matches the curve of the turret base, then use putty to fair it into the hull top. There are two more fairings behind the projection of the glacis above the hull top, and they are made up from 10 thou sheet. The stowage boxes, filler caps etc can all be reproduced with sheet plastic. On either side there is also a large cover for the exhaust system, which is a characteristic of the later Conquerors. These are built from pieces of 40 thou sheet which, when assembled, are filed to shape.

The model is now ready for painting. There is little choice available here, as the Conqueror tanks were almost invariably painted in the standard British Army deep bronze green. Number plates were carried front and rear, and BAOR vehicles had a Union Jack painted on the Infantry telephone box on the upper left of the hull rear. There were three reflectors spaced equally along the lower edge of the rear plate, but other items such as bridging discs (bearing the figure '80' to indicate the very heavy class of bridge needed to carry the Conqueror's weight) and Royal Armoured Corps flashes were variable in position and often not carried. The model illustrated has a smart 'parade-ground' finish which is typical of the Conquerors seen in photographs. They fought in no wars and so, apart from an occasional exercise, were normally maintained in a reasonably tidy condition; also, with their great size, there was less call to stow baggage externally. If you choose to model this appearance, it is worth taking extra care over the painting of the model, to obtain an even and smooth finish. This will leave you with an impressive replica of the largest tank ever to see service with the British Army. □

THE CONGREVE ROCKET SYSTEM

Stuart Asquith describes these famous Napoleonic weapons and how to model them for wargames

The RHA Rocket Troop is seldom if ever seen represented on the Napoleonic wargames table. The inclusion of such a unit in a British army would add a certain amount of interest, underlined by its rarity value and inherent unreliability.

Rockets first appeared on the British military scene in the early part of the 19th Century. Colonel William Congreve, eldest son of the Comptroller of the Royal Laboratory, Woolwich, was an officer in the Hanoverian army. Congreve was interested in the reports from the Honourable East India Company's troops sent to quell a rising in Mysore in 1792, that they met more than they bargained for. Tippoo Sultaun, one of the rebelling Maharatta's leaders, was a great user of rockets, and certainly company reports showed that troops suffered more from the rockets than from the guns of the enemy, a view supported by the Adjutant General of the East India Company.

The Board of Ordnance in London was also interested in the military possibilities of rockets and prompted by such reports enquired at the Royal Laboratory for an expert. None was forthcoming and it was Congreve himself who offered his services. Official interest in rockets seems to have been short-lived, however, and Congreve was soon left to his own devices and expenses.

He quickly appreciated the better points of the rocket as a projectile: its lightness and the fact that it needed no charge for it to be able to fire, as did contemporary artillery pieces. During the early 1800s he experimented with various rockets, ranging in weight from 6 lb to 32 lb with sticks of different lengths up to a maximum of 15 feet, with a diameter of 1½ inches.

The rockets saw action at the attack on Boulogne Harbour (1806), Copenhagen (1807) and at Leipzig (1813). In the Peninsula too, the rockets distinguished themselves at the crossing of the River Adour (1814). In passing it should also be noted that rockets were used on several occasions during the War of 1812 against America with reasonable success. Rockets were also present at Waterloo in 1815 but did not play a really significant role in the battle. It can be seen, however, there is ample historical support for any wargame rocket battery, since the British use of the rocket crops up with reasonable frequency throughout the Napoleonic Wars.

The main usage of the military rocket was against fortifications and, to a lesser extent, against the wooden shipping of the period. Containing as they did an incendiary composition of sulphur and tallow, rockets were ideal for setting buildings on fire. The flight path, however, could not be determined with any degree of accuracy and rockets were never very popular with the British Army as a whole. One useful side effect of the rocket was its adverse effect on morale. Cavalry were certainly disrupted by rocket fire and at Leipzig an entire brigade of

Below left *The RHA officer used straight from the Airfix box.* **Below right** *Two RHA gunners with rocket sticks added prior to painting* (all photos by Alan Wright).

infantry surrendered after a couple of minute's barrage from the Rocket Troop.

It was not until January 1813 that 'Rocket Detachments' were added to the strength of the RHA. In 1814 the 1st and 2nd Rocket Troops emerged after a minor re-shuffle. The 1st troop was commanded by Captain Elliott and the 2nd by Captain Whinyates. The Duke of Wellington was never very keen on the Rocket Troops and indeed early in 1815 tried to convert the 2nd troop into horse artillery. It was not until Sir George Wood, commanding the artillery in the Duke's Army, intervened, that Captain Whinyates was allowed to retain at least some of his 12 pdr rockets.

As well as gaining the battle honour 'Waterloo' the 2nd Rocket Troop was given the honour 'Leipsic' to commemorate their part in the battle as the only British unit present. Ironically enough in 1816 the 2nd Rocket Troop was disbanded and its two honours went to the 1st Troop which in the event had never left England.

Organisation

The Rocket Troops were organised in much the same manner as the conventional Horse Artillery Troops. The Troop consisted of three divisions each of two sub-divisions. A sub-division had five sections each of three troops and two drivers, leading four ammunition horses. All men were mounted and each carried four rounds of 12 pdr rocket ammunition, with each ammunition horse carrying 18 rounds. Each sub-division carried five *bouches a feu,* small iron troughs some 18 inches long which were used to fire rockets from the ground. Also attached were two horse-drawn 'Rocket Cars', one heavy carrying four men and 40 x 24 pdr rockets, one light carrying two men and 60 x 12 pdr rockets.

The complete troop then consisted of 102 mounted men, 24 ammunition horses, carrying 30 *bouches a feu* and 840 rounds of ammunition, increased to 940 with the inclusion of the cars. In addition to all this, Congreve proposed the use of

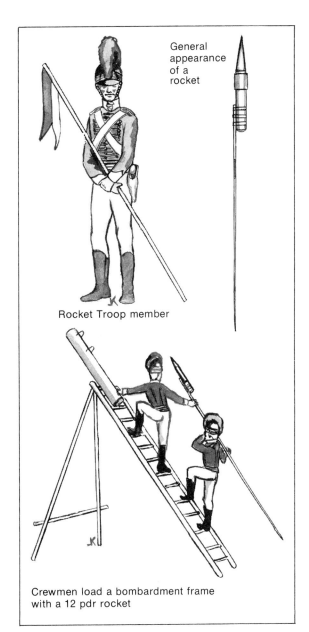

General appearance of a rocket

Rocket Troop member

Crewmen load a bombardment frame with a 12 pdr rocket

Below *Two RHA officers converted into Rocket Troop members with scratch-built rocket box.* **Below right** *The scratch-built bombardment frame.*

ammunition carts to supplement the carrying of the rockets. Having a capacity of 60 rounds, they normally carried most of the equipment of the mounted troops, rocket sticks and three out of the four rockets each man carried. In action, however, each trooper reverted to his scheduled load and the carts were able to increase the ammunition supply to 200 rounds per sub-division all told. A further reserve of ammunition was left with the main artillery park.

The rockets themselves were in three main groups:

		Length of stick	Range in yards
Heavy	8″ diameter carcass (body) explosion rocket	24′	2,500-7,000
	7″ diameter carcass (body) explosion rocket	23′ 3″	2,500-7,000
	6″ diameter carcass (body) explosion rocket	21′ 9″	2,500-7,000
Medium	42 pdr carcass	18′	3,000
	32 pdr carcass or shell	15′	3,000
	24 pdr shell or case	14′	3,000
Light	18 pdr shell or case shot	13′	2,500
	12 pdr shell or case shot	9′ 6″	2,500
	9 pdr shell or case shot	9′ 6″	2,200
	6 pdr shell	9′	2,200

The most frequently used were the 24 pdr (which Congreve likened to a 12 pdr shot) mainly in a bombardment role and the light group of rockets for general field work.

Modelling notes

The obvious source of figures for the plastic modeller is the Airfix 'British Artillery at Waterloo' set. Each box of figures yields eight gunners in action poses, with two limber riders and four mounted figures. Two guns, a limber and seven horses are also provided.

Initially, then, let us consider the actual crewmen. It is pre-supposed the wargamer will want the rocket depicted in a firing position, so active crew members will be required. Minor conversions only are needed to turn the RHA gunners into rocket crew members, since the bulk of the Airfix figures are already in action poses. Basically the choice of poses is up to the individual, but obviously those with rammers and the like lend themselves to easy conversion. For the rocket sticks I used scale lengths of fine piano wire — after heating the wire it is simply pressed against the figure. The hands melt quickly due to the heat of the wire and, given a bit of luck, reform around it.

A couple of figures, the officer with telescope and the trooper 'lighting' the gun can be used as they are, but obviously the fuse for a rocket should be considerably longer than the one depicted on the gunner as issued. A piece of fine black cotton will fit the bill nicely, although if this is glued in place both on the rocket and the trooper it makes for a very fragile finished model.

The 'double' figure set carrying a box of rocket heads were originally officers looking through telescopes. In this case the piano wire was pressed on the figures' shoulders after the telescopes were cut away. This then gives the impression of a load

Above left *Scratch-built rocket cart, prior to filling and painting.* **Left** *Mounted member of the Rocket Troop.*

Ammunition horse

View of completed model — the base has been kept simple for better display of the frame and figures.

being lifted on the figures' shoulders. The box was simply balsa cut to scale from the spares box, as were the wire handles holding the box on the carrying rod.

On examination of a set of the RHA Airfix figures many more equally simple conversions will immediately become obvious to the modeller. Perhaps the figure depicted with two buckets should be painted up and kept available — bearing in mind the unreliability of the rockets!

Obviously, in order to have an effective-looking wargame rocket troop it is necessary to model not only the crewmen but also some of their equipment. Hopefully the accompanying diagrams adequately explain the method of construction of both the rocket cart and the bombardment frames.

In the case of the rocket cart the chassis is simply made by turning upside down one of the gun carriages from the Waterloo British Artillery set. For extra strength a drawing pin was pushed through the bottom of the cart into the gun carriage, thus giving a very steady base on which to build. It was then a case of cutting the plywood (balsa would serve equally well) to size and gluing the sections together.

The bombardment frame was a little more tricky. After several failures to satisfactorily produce the rocket firing tube at the top of the frame, grooves were substituted in which to locate the rockets in a firing position. The ladder used by the crewmen to reach the firing tube can pose problems, but that from the Airfix 'Commando' set of figures is ideal. The only problem here was that the ladder had no strength in itself and I was forced to support it with a platform as shown in the sketch. The finished effect, however, was accurate enough, and looked to be a fair representation of the original.

I felt that the *bouches a feu* were too small for accurate construction in 25 mm scale. Several prototypes were tried, but even the best effort was quashed when a wargame opponent enquired if the

British had accidentally dropped some rockets on the table.

Rocket cars have not been modelled in detail, since accurate information on them is limited. It was felt, however, that use of the limbers from the ever-faithful British Artillery box would fit the bill nicely, together with the horses from the same set. The rockets themselves were simply pieces of sprue carved to a point, with tails of piano wire cut to scale lengths. The ammunition horses can be fairly easily made. A nearly static horse pose was chosen from the Airfix 'Wagon Train' set. This had the bonus of having more or less the correct harness already depicted on the animal. The pack was built up in Plasticine and sculpted until it was a fair representation of the horse shown in the sketch.

Wargame usage

It is never a good idea to present rigid rules to wargamers. Any rules must necessarily be based on one person's interpretation of what actually happened on the field of battle. By their very nature, then, such rules when laid down are open to disagreement and debate by fellow wargamers; and why not? On such discussions surely the hobby thrives? Several points have to be borne in mind, however, when formulating rules for the use of rockets.

Firstly, rockets were notoriously unpredictable once fired, so rules should allow for this. It would appear that rockets had much the same theoretical range as their artillery counterparts so the wargame ranges should be similar. One method of simulating the rocket's inaccuracy is to break the flight path down into sections and dice for the direction of the rocket in that section. An example of this would be to take a range of some 36 inches

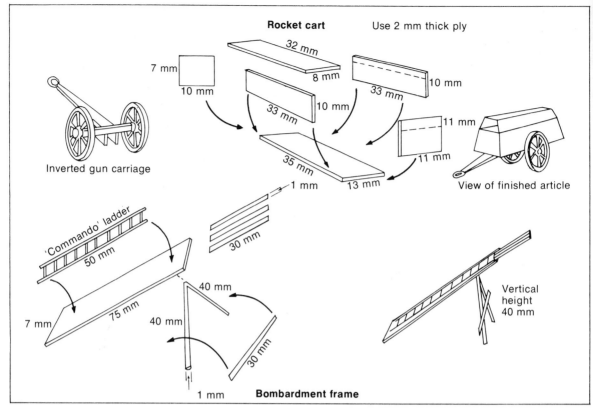

Rocket cart   Use 2 mm thick ply

7 mm

10 mm

32 mm

8 mm

33 mm   10 mm

33 mm   10 mm

11 mm

11 mm

35 mm

1 mm   13 mm

View of finished article

Inverted gun carriage

'Commando' ladder

50 mm

30 mm

7 mm   75 mm   40 mm

40 mm

40 mm

30 mm

Vertical height 40 mm

1 mm   **Bombardment frame**

and divide it into six sections each of six inches. A dice is thrown for each section and the following table referred to: Score of 1 — rocket blows up at once; 2 — shoots vertically upwards; 3 — veers 90° left; 4 — veers 90° right; 5 — hits ground at end of section; 6 — carries on straight. Obviously a wider range of possibilities could be created by using two dice or even percentage dice, but the principle would remain. It will be a very lucky wargamer who gets his rockets on target at the end of all that dice throwing.

What of the effect when the rocket does land, intentionally or otherwise? This again depends on the wargamer's own personal rules as to whether burst circle indicators are used or casualties are diced for, with or without saving throws. The bursting effect of the rocket is perhaps best represented

by using rules normally applicable to shell fire, with casualties being allotted accordingly.

One of the main benefits of rockets was their incendiary effect on buildings, etc, and it is unlikely that the average Napoleonic wargamer has adequate rules for such situations. Probably it would be sufficient as a general rule to stipulate that any building hit by a rocket will be set on fire and will burn for 'x' number of moves. Naturally, much will depend on the size of the building in question, be it cathedral or cottage, but that can be safely left to the wargamer's discretion, after all we are all sensible fellows at heart . . .

Finally the rocket's effect on morale should be considered — cavalry mounts were somewhat unnerved by rockets whooshing over them. Suffice to say that any units the rocket's flight crosses should have an immediate morale test — normal rules applying. Note of course the British commander's own men may well have to check morale, should the rocket go astray.

In closing I must admit I have had varying degrees of success using a rocket battery in my own British Napoleonic army. In one glorious action Napoleon and his entire staff were felled by one well-aimed missile; regrettably, however, in a subsequent battle Wellington very nearly received the same treatment. Still, the inclusion of a Rocket Battery will add a fresh element into an immensely popular wargame period and may even produce a few premature grey hairs among its users! □

Horse team and limber used as rocket car, with crewman, prior to painting.

LEANDERS FOR SALE

Paul Beaver outlines the British shipbuilding industry's export 'Leander' programme

The USN-style numerals show up well in this photograph of HMAS Torrens. Note the Dutch radar on the fore and main masts, plus the Ikara director on the bridge top (RAN via Paul Beaver).

For many years, the United Kingdom reigned supreme in world shipbuilding. Today, as we all sadly know, there is a slump in trade especially in the mercantile market. However, what is perhaps not so generally known is that Britain is one of the world's leading naval shipbuilding nations and exporters.

In the last few years, British companies such as Vosper Thornycroft, Yarrow, Vickers and Brooke Marine have successfully exported warships to many nations, including Argentina, Brazil, Brunei and Malaysia. Since World War 2, the most successful class of 'grey ship' to be designed and built in Britain has been the ubiquitous 'Leander' Class frigate, the Improved Type 12. The Royal Navy (RN) ordered 26 of these general purpose frigates and

these have subsequently been divided into three sub-groups: namely the Ikara (for anti-submarine warfare or ASW), the Exocet (for surface strike) and the standard Gun type. The Class is of course well known to millions of viewers of the BBC TV *Warship* series.

The Leander has also been a leading export earner since the early 1960s, not only in terms of equipment and actual ships, but also in several instances the actual naval design skills have been exported. Three Commonwealth Navies, one NATO partner and a nation in South America, have all found a useful slot in their Fleets for the Leander, to the tune of some 16 units. Each nation's Leander contingent is analysed below.

Way 'down-under', the Royal Australian Navy (RAN) operates in the basic United States Navy (USN) fashion and hence a frigate is actually termed a Destroyer Escort (DE). Both HM Australian Ships *Swan* (DE50) and *Torrens* (DE53) were laid down in Australia on August 18 1965. The former was built

Built on the Clyde, HMNZS Canterbury *is one of two ordered from British yards by the New Zealand government. Several differences between RNZN and RN 'Leanders' are apparent here (Yarrow Shipbuilders).*

at the Naval Dockyard in Williamstoun, Victoria and the latter at Cockatoo Docks in Sydney. Both these warships joined the Third Destroyer Squadron and their four sister ships *Derwent, Parramatta, Stuart* and *Yarra;* the latter, although also members of the 'River' Class in RAN eyes, are really similar to the older 'Rothesay' Class design.

It will be apparent, when studying photographs of the two Australian ships, that they have more than a passing resemblance to the 'Van Speijk' Class of the Royal Netherlands Navy (RNN). This is due mainly to the use of similar surveillance radar, the HSA (Hollandse Signaalapparaten) LW O2 which replaces the Type 965 RN radar on the mainmast. On the foremast head can be found the ball-type HSA M 20 target sensor which immediately identifies a Leander as being Australian. Another purely-RAN difference, readily apparent to the observer and especially to the modeller, is the lack of flight deck, helicopter hangar and Variable Depth Sonar (VDS) well. The *Swan* and *Torrens* rely for ASW on the Limbo mortar aft and the Ikara ASW missile which is positioned on the after superstructure. Modellers will recall that the RN Ikara-refits have the system forward of the bridge, replacing the 114 mm gun turret. The Ikara guidance radome is situated directly on top of the bridge.

In Australian service then the 'Leander' Class frigates are primarily employed as anti-submarine escorts with a fairly limited surface strike capabili-

ty, rather than a jack-of-all-trades general purpose frigate. For air defence, in common with all Leanders, the 'River' Class uses the now ageing 'Seacat' SAM system, and it will be interesting to see which other navies follow the RN line and refit with Seawolf in the 1980s.

Moving across the Tasman Sea to the Antipodes, the small Royal New Zealand Navy (RNZN) was in fact one of the first export customers for the Leander. HMNZS *Waikato* (F55) was laid down on January 10 1964 at the Harland and Wolff yard at Belfast and she was commissioned on September 19 1966. She then commenced sea trials in UK water and whilst on passage to New Zealand, where she arrived in May 1967. Since being built she has been considerably altered aft of the funnel following a refit and she bears only a small resemblance to the outline of her sister ship HMNZS *Canterbury* (F421). Incidentally, RNZN warships are painted a lighter grey than their RN counterparts and this colour is termed 'Waikato grey'. Modellers should note also that New Zealand warships do not have a white surround to their black pennant numbers.

So successful was the *Waikato,* that the New Zealand Government decided, in August 1968, to order a follow-up sister-ship, to be built this time at the lead-yard at Yarrow's on the Clyde. HMNZS *Canterbury* was laid down on April 12 1969 and completed in the autumn of 1971. In the meantime Britain lent New Zealand HMS *Blackpool* (F77), now a target ship, as a stop gap. *Canterbury* is basically a standard Gun-type Leander with the twin 114 mm gun turret, British radars and a large flight deck. The latter feature is possible because both the mortar and VDS wells are not included in the design. It

Above HMNZS Canterbury *on review at Spithead in June 1977.* **Below** HMNZS Canterbury's *flight deck is of large size and can easily accommodate her Wasp ASW helicopter.*

Above *The Chilean 'Leander' Condell on the Clyde during builder's trials. Note the stern-mounted Exocet missile launchers (Yarrow Shipbuilders via Paul Beaver).* **Below** *The name ship of the Dutch 'Leander' Class, HNLMS Van Speijk. Note the Wasp on deck and Dutch radars (Koninklijke Marine via Paul Beaver).*

is ironic that while the RN and the RNN are busily converting their Leanders to take the large Lynx ASW helicopter, the RNZN has no plans to purchase this helicopter but *Canterbury* has the deck to use it.

A noticeable recognition feature of RNZN Leanders is the black kiwi emblem on the funnel, plus the fact that *Canterbury* also has triple ASW torpedo tubes and extended funnel vents. *Waikato* has neither of these features, but she retains the Limbo mortar.

For many years, one of Britain's major seafaring allies has been the Netherlands and this is apparent by the amount of compatibility between the Dutch and British Navies — even the uniforms look alike.

In October 1962, the Dutch Government decided to order replacements for the 'Van Amstel' Class. These replacement frigates were given the name 'Van Speijk' Class after a famous Dutch naval hero. They are based on the Leander design although they have small modifications built into the design by the Netherlands United Shipbuilding Bureaux. It was decided, in order to avoid any delay and to give employment at home, that, as far as possible, Dutch equipment would be used. Naturally this causes a difference in appearance of the Class as compared with their British cousins. As with the RAN's 'River' Class, HSA radars have been used; on the mainmast is the same LW O2 surveillance radar as mentioned earlier, with a DA O5 target indicator and a pair of M-44 reflectors as with the RAN and Indian Navy ships. Finally, the gun turret training is controlled by an M-45 director on top of the bridge.

At present, 1977-82, the Class is under progressive modernization refits to replace the main turret with a single Oto-Melara 76/62 mm 'Compact' gun turret (similar in shape to the Vickers Mk 8 114 mm turret) and to install the US Sea Harpoon canister launched missile system amidships. Additional items include the provision of twin triple-torpedo tubes and a new radar on the foremast of HSA design, incorporating IFF sensors. The rear flight deck is to be enlarged, by presumably plating over the Limbo mortar well, to enable the Class to operate the Lynx SH-14A helicopter in the 1980s.

The original construction of the Class was undertaken by yards in Amsterdam and Flushing on an equal basis, and the nameship of the Class, HNLMS *Van Speijk* (F802) was laid down on October 1 1963 and completed on February 14 1967. The last two ships completed, HNLM Ships *Isaac Sweers* (F814) and *Evertsen* (F815) were ordered a little later than the original four and they were not commissioned until 1968. All six are frequent visitors to the UK on exercise and goodwill visits.

In January 1970, Chile joined in the South American arms race with an order for one, later supplemented by another 'Leander' Class frigate. The two frigates, named *Condell* (PF06) and *Lynch* (PF07), have caused much political controversy and, although they were built in Britain, exact details are difficult to come by. Both ships are well

The dark grey Indian 'Leander' Udaygiri *at the Spithead review in June 1977.*

armed with twin 114 mm guns, two 20 mm Oerlikon (another standard Leander fitment), twin triple-torpedo tubes, a flight deck with associated hangar, and perhaps most interesting of all, the Limbo and VDS wells have been replaced by four Exocet launchers. This latter positioning gives the Chilean Navy more flexibility in the surface strike situation. The only major change to the superstructure appears to be the higher foremast.

Finally, a Navy which is still building up its fleet of Leanders is India. The Indian Leander Programme spans more than ten years and is still not completed. The first ship in the Class was laid down in October 1966 at Mazagon Docks, Bombay, becoming the first major surface unit to be constructed in India. INS *Nilgiri* (F32) is basically similar to RN Leanders with UK radars, a single Seacat SAM with a GWS22 director. Later ships in the Class, *Himgiri* (F33), *Dunagiri* (F34), *Udaygiri* (F35), *Taragiri* (F36) and *Vindhyadagiri* (F37), have been equipped with two Seacats and HSA directors, plus standard HSA radars. Other equipment includes Limbo mortars, VDS and provision for an Alouette III ASW helicopter. This later necessitated an extended hangar and the flight deck, dark grey in colour, exhibits distinct Dayglo markings. The whole ship is painted a dark grey colour with white pennant, squadron numbers, and flight deck codes.

Representative Flight Deck Codes

	Pen No	Code	Helicopter
HMNZS *Canterbury*	F421	CA	Wasp HAS 1
HNLMS *Van Speijk*	F802	VS	Wasp AH-12A
HNLMS *Van Nes*	F805	VN	Wasp AH-12A
INS *Udaygiri*	F35	DD	Alouette III

On exercise in the North Sea with other units of the Royal Netherlands Navy is the Isaac Sweers, *the penultimate Dutch 'Leander'* (Koninklijke Marine via Paul Beaver).

Naturally this survey has not been in great depth, but it is hoped that it will encourage modellers to consider producing foreign variants of the Leander kit, which is available from Airfix. Further reference can be made to *Jane's Fighting Ships* for technical data.

The author wishes to thank the following for their kind assistance: Yarrow (Shipbuilders) Ltd, *Alle Hens* Magazine, the Netherlands United Shipbuilding Bureaux, the Royal Australian, Netherlands and New Zealand Navies, Les Marriage and F. J. Bachofner of IPMS, and MOD(Navy). ☐

Leander Quick Reference

Name	Pen No	Navy	Details	Completion/ Commissioned
Swan	DE50	RAN	114 mm gun; Ikara; Limbo; Seacat	January 20 1970
Torrens	DE53	RAN	114 mm gun; Ikara; Limbo; Seacat	January 19 1971
Waikato	F55	RNZN	114 mm gun; Seacat; Limbo; Wasp	September 19 1966
Canterbury	F421	RNZN	114 mm gun; Seacat; ASW torpedoes; Wasp	October 22 1971
Van Speijk	F802	RNN	114 mm gun; Seacat; Wasp; Limbo; VDS	February 14 1967
Van Galen	F803	RNN	114 mm gun; Seacat; Wasp; Limbo; VDS	March 1 1967
Tjerk Hiddes	F804	RNN	114 mm gun; Seacat; Wasp; Limbo; VDS	August 16 1967
Van Nes	F805	RNN	114 mm gun; Seacat; Wasp; Limbo; VDS	August 9 1967
Isaac Sweers	F814	RNN	114 mm gun; Seacat; Wasp; Limbo; VDS	May 15 1968
Evertsen	F815	RNN	114 mm gun; Seacat; Wasp; Limbo; VDS	December 21 1967
Condell	PF06	ChN	114 mm gun; Seacat; ASW torpedoes; Exocet	December 21 1973
Lynch	PF07	ChN	114 mm gun; Seacat; ASW torpedoes; Exocet	May 25 1974
Dunagiri	F34	IN	114 mm gun; Seacat; Limbo; VDS; Alouette	1976
Himgiri	F33	IN	114 mm gun; Seacat; Limbo; VDS; Alouette	November 1974
Nilgiri	F32	IN	114 mm gun; Seacat; Limbo; VDS; Alouette	June 1972
Udaygiri	F35	IN	114 mm gun; Seacat; Limbo; VDS; Alouette	1975
Taragiri	F36	IN	—	—
Vindhydagiri	F37	IN	—	—

STUKAS IN THE SUN!

John Sandars describes how to model the 40 mm Bofors AA gun in 1:32 scale

Wartime photo on which gun detachment figures and some details of the gun were based.

The Swedish-designed 40 mm Bofors was the standard British Light Anti-Aircraft Gun throughout World War 2, as well as being used by many other countries then and since. Light Ack-Ack regiments had three batteries each with three troops of up to six guns apiece. One such regiment formed part of each armoured and infantry division, while others served in the AA brigades as Corps and Army troops and in AA Command in UK. Most guns were mobile, towed first by Morris CD/SW tractors and later by Bedford QLBs. In North-West Europe

towards the end of the war some regiments had one battery of self-propelled Bofors guns on the unarmoured Morris C9/B vehicle, while the Crusader AA tank Mk I also mounted a Bofors in an armoured open-topped turret. Many of the guns were fitted for control by a Kerrison predictor which was often used, particularly on static sites.

There were three main marks of gun, over a dozen marks of mounting of various types, and five different designs of firing platform produced in Britain alone. I do not pretend to know what combination of these make up the gun depicted in the model; suffice it to say it was an early type used in the Desert without the gunshield, later improved sighting gear, or the electric drives for the predic-

Above *Bofors emplacement in the desert which gave the idea of the gunpit, ammunition boxes, nets, mugs, etc, in the model.* **Below** *Overall view of gun showing towing bogie and portable legs of firing platform fitted.*

tor. In fact it was one of the simpler possible variations.

The information for making the model came almost entirely from photographs, but overall dimensions were obtained from books and by scaling up measurements from a 1:76 scale drawing in *Tankette.* (Nowadays the Airfix kit could be used.) Some help was also obtained from a rather rough and undetailed metal kit of a 1:32 scale gun which was the same scale as the model I was making. Photographs of the gun with its detachment in action or at drill are pretty easy to come by since they could be taken at home or behind the front

lines abroad, and many wartime books and magazines, as well as more recent publications such as the Macdonald & Jane's *Fact Files* contain good examples.

The actual pictures which inspired the model, and shown here, were found on a loose page from an old magazine — origin unknown. As can be seen this sort of picture is fine for making a diorama with a kit-built model since it gives the 'feel' of the scene, and shows how the gun detachment would be positioned, clothed, etc. Although such general photographs may well show bits of detail even a large number may not show enough between them to make a large-scale scratch-built model. For this close-up detail pictures of an actual gun are better (supposing, as here, detail drawings are not available). Obtaining these is not as difficult as it may sound, provided you are prepared to take your own, as there are several World War 2 Bofors guns still around; there is one outside the Rotunda at Woolwich and another in the Imperial War Museum, for example. The two that were photographed for this 1/32 scale model were from private collections and were snapped, on the off chance that the pictures might be useful one day, during military vehicle rallies at Warnham and Shottesbrooke a couple of years ago. As can be seen neither is exactly the type of equipment modelled, nor are they still complete in all respects, but when used in conjunction with 'action' illustrations in books and magazines a full picture can be built up.

It is difficult to interpret pictures to scratch-build a model without having some idea as to how the original works. Externally the Bofors was fairly simple and the pictures and drawings in this article

Above left *Another general view of the gun. Elevating gear and firing pedal can be seen.* **Above right** *Training gear and empty cartridge chute can be seen here. Shield and this type of barrel clamp (in foreground) are not fitted on the model.* **Below left** *Gun platform detail. Portable legs can be seen in their stowed position, also pickets, jacks, part of firing gear linkage under breech and brackets for pickets on legs.* **Below right** *Firing platform and mounting turntable. The bracket for cleaning rods can be seen on the back of the loader's platform, and the mounting for the quick traverse handle (missing) on supports to the used cartridge chute.*

should give all the information required, but one or two points may need a little elucidation. Ammunition is held together in batches of four rounds by steel clips fitted down one side of the bases of the cartridges. These are loaded with the clip on the left (facing the muzzle) and it is then ejected through the slot that can be seen below the rear of the Autoloader on that side. The curved lever pivoted below and in front of this operated the mechanism by hand. The two side pieces of the mounting are secured to the top of the turntable by two flat metal beams; under the ends of these, which protrude beyond the turntable, the tubular framework which carries the loader's platform, and the layer's seats and footrests, is secured.

The two balance cylinders under the barrel are pivoted at the front of the mounting side pieces, and the piston rods that move in and out of them as the gun elevates and depresses are secured to

either side of the elevating quadrant fixed beneath the breech. The two firing pedals, one by the aimer's right foot and the other to the left of the cartridge chute on the loader's platform, are linked by rods and operate a small rocking arm which pushes on a pin from the firing mechanism which sticks out from the centre of the left trunnion. The lever at the back of the loader's platform (not shown on the pictures of the actual guns) is for quick traversing; links from its left and right ends held up the firing pedal and disengaged the traversing gear respectively when it was depressed, and the No 1, standing on the ground behind the gun, could then use it to swing the whole mounting quickly on to the line of a new target. Brackets on the back of the platform below this carry the cleaning rod in sections. The circular bolted blanks on the gearboxes below the elevating and traversing cranks are where the electric drives, presumably

for military modellers

from the predictor, would be connected if they were fitted.

The lower part of the turntable is bolted to a hollow octagon box with oval limber holes in the sides carrying the fixed fore and aft, and portable side legs of the firing platform. At the forward end of the rectangular fixed leg a pivoting block with side stops fits over the single bearing in the axle of the bogie with the tow bar. (Note: in the above description of the gun and mounting left and right are taken, as usual, facing the muzzle, but since the gun travels muzzle aft, from here on and on the drawing of the complete assembly the front corresponds to the breech end of the gun.) At the back a rigid cross piece holds the two bearings of the trailing bogie, on which the brake is mounted. This is operated by a lanyard passed around a pulley on the brake arm and led forward via a vertical eye on the bogie, a toggle joint and an horizontal eye on the firing platform, to a cleat on the front leg of same. The hinged barrel clamp is secured by spring catches to the block holding the small cylinder beneath the recoil spring cover. (On the model the slots in this cover and the spring within it have been omitted since a dust cover was to be added obscuring them.)

The two tubular portable legs are shown, one shipped and one stowed on the drawing; when the gun is emplaced both should, of course, be shipped, and the 'T' section pickets, stowed either side of the front fixed leg, could be driven down through the brackets on the ends of all four legs and into

---

Top left *Front view showing elevating pinion and arc, balance cylinders, front of cartridge chute and portable legs fitted.* **Above left** *General view showing details of training, crank and ammunition clips.* **Left** *Trailing axle showing brake unit (barrel clamp not as fitted on model).* **Below** *Constituent parts of the model ready for assembly.*

Above photos *Finished model of gun in travelling configuration before being 'emplaced' on its base.* **Below right** *Gun and roughed-out figures offered up before finishing.*

the ground, but this does not seem to have been done very often except on more or less permanent sites. They have been left stowed on the model.

No drawing was needed to make the model; the one with this article was prepared afterwards from the finished item and is *not* 100 per cent accurate. (If any 'rivet counters' feel in danger of a heart attack at this point they should read no further!) The reason for this is twofold; first, there are, of course, unavoidable minor dimensional errors when making a model without a proper engineering drawing to start from, and second, standard diameter plastic rod and tube has been used for outriggers, jacks, balance cylinders, etc, and a convenient punch used for the holes in the jack plates and seats, none of which are exactly the right size. Similarly the barrel, which is the handle of a mapping pen with a piece of paintbrush handle for the flash eliminator on the muzzle, is a little thick, and the ammunition, which is from cocktail sticks sanded down while being spun in a battery-operated hand drill, is also a bit on the fat side.

All this is deliberate since it was reckoned that a model of this sort would look better and more realistic if parts that should be round and smoothly finished were in fact so, even if slightly the wrong size, rather than being whittled down by hand with a less satisfactory finish in order to achieve greater dimensional accuracy. It is after all a 'modeller's' model intended to give the feel of the scene and look authentic, not an 'engineer's' model to be checked with a micrometer.

for military modellers

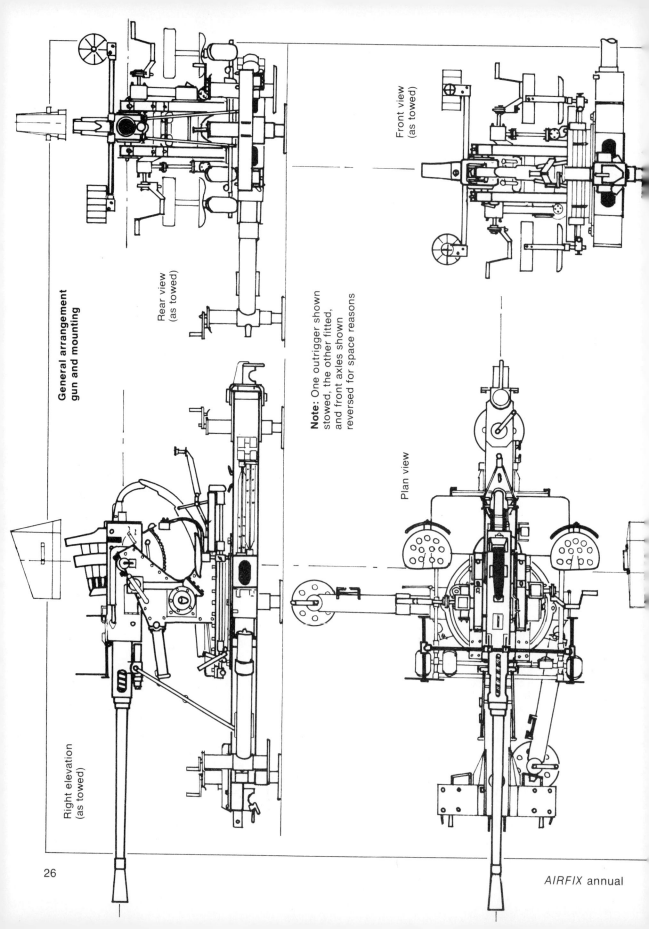

General arrangement gun and mounting

Rear view (as towed)

Front view (as towed)

Right elevation (as towed)

Plan view

Note: One outrigger shown stowed, the other fitted, and front axles shown reversed for space reasons

AIRFIX annual

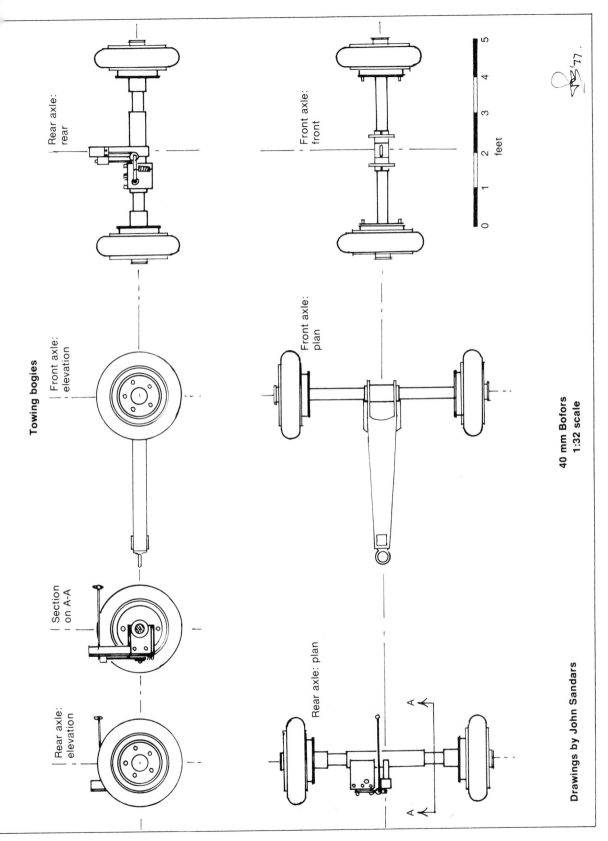

Towing bogies

Rear axle: rear

Front axle: front

feet

Front axle: elevation

Front axle: plan

Section on A-A

Rear axle: elevation

Rear axle: plan

A

A

**40 mm Bofors
1:32 scale**

Drawings by John Sandars

Above *The completed model (see also colour photo).*
Right *Some of the detachment figures completed. The man on the left is carved from a Multipose figure, that in the centre has Tamiya torso between Multipose head and legs, and that on the right has a tissue 'jersey' over a basic Multipose torso. Note lengthened shorts (left) and strings for ID tags around necks. Shells are yellow with red bands.*

Apart from the tyres, which were rubber ones from a toy (as they proved a little too thin to cast in resin by the method I usually use without warping), the whole model was scratch-built using cardboard, balsa wood coated with paper and various gauges of plastic rod and tube. The sights, perhaps the most delicate parts, were made up from fuse wire rings and very fine plastic rod stuck with Loctite 'Superglue' and a certain amount of patience. The figures are a mixture of Airfix Multipose and Tamiya 25 pdr gun detachment figures. This was because of the lack of figures with bare torsos available when the model was made. One 'bare' figure was carved and built up from the Multipose alone, but the others used torso and arms from Tamiya with a 'heightening' strip of about 1 mm inserted at the waistband. Legs and heads were all Airfix. The gunpit, admittedly made a little smaller than real due to size of base and display problems, was built up of individual sandbags (nearly 70 all together) made from Plasticine wrapped in tissue. The ammo boxes were wood covered with cardboard. The basic paint scheme on the gun should be similar to 'unbleached linen', with thinned and darkened Dark Earth run into the various cracks and crevices, and the whole dry-brushed first with Dark Earth and then an 'unbleached wool' shade. Airfix paints provide all the necessary colours.

The plan, photographs and this brief description should make it possible for anyone who wishes to make up a similar Bofors of their own, although such is the timelag between writing and printing that a large-scale kit of the gun might well be on the market by the time you read this. Even so the article may provide ideas for other models for those of us who still prefer the do-it-yourself approach, rather than sticking kits together, however good they are! □

17th Lancers 1829~1832

Bryan and Don Fosten describe the uniforms of this élite light cavalry unit

At this time the 17th Lancers (The Duke of Cambridge's Own) had, as its Colonel, Lieutenant General Sir John Elley, KCB, KCH who was the Member of Parliament for Windsor in 1835. A series of drawings by G. E. Salisbury give an excellent picture of the uniform of the regiment about 1829, and these have provided the basis for the following description of the uniform of the regiment for the period under review.

Officer in Levée dress

The headdress is the *tschapska,* the Polish style trencher-top lance cap. This period saw the headdress very high-waisted with a wide flat top. The skull was black and the caned top covered in white cloth. The upper white part was separated from the black lower half by a wide band of silver lace with a central blue stripe. The outside edges of this lace band were scalloped and there was a narrower band of silver lace placed about an inch below the wider band with a thin strip of the black skull part visible between.

The sharply sloped black leather visor of the cap was edged with three bands of silver lace and the back was reinforced by a *couvre-nuque* of black stout leather with a silver lace decorative band edged on either side with a blue stripe. The silver chin scales were suspended from large lions' heads and the frontal cap plate was very large with a gilt rayed edge and a central silver ornament consisting of the Full Royal Coat of Arms with the Regimental Badge — the Death's-head and Crossed Bones and label lettered 'OR GLORY' beneath. On the left side of the upper front edge was a richly padded gold lace cockade with a white velvet centre decorated with the Royal Cypher from which a very large white swans' feather drooping plume over crimson dyed feathers was fixed.

Salisbury indicates that the jacket was dark-blue, made very tight, with a high white cloth 'Prussian' collar, narrow, shaped lapels, pointed cuffs and tiny Polish turnbacks. The coat had silver buttons. The red Morocco leather pouch belt was covered with silver lace with a very narrow white cloth stripe down the centre and showing the suspicion of the red leather on the outside edges. The pouch belt had silver pickers and chains from a silver lion's head. The collar and cuffs of the jacket were decorated with silver lace, and on each shoulder were large silver embroidered epaulettes with silver crescents on white cloth with silver, blue lined bridles. The girdle was gold lace with two crimson stripes. The officer wears an elaborate silver aigulette on the left shoulder looped across in some ill-defined way to the right shoulder. The pantaloons were blue, made close fitting to the leg, and had a broad silver stripe down the outside of each leg.

Major A. McK. Annand has described the portrait of Cornet Charles Forbes of the Regiment by J. J. Masquerier circa 1825. The uniform shown in this magnificent painting is very similar to the description given above. Major Annand comments on the lance cap shown in the painting. It has a top, ten inches square, with fluted sides and gold cord running up the corners. The plume is called 'a drooping white and red cocktail plume' which was shortly to be changed to a plume of swans' feathers in accordance with the Regulations of 1826. Cornet Forbes has gold cap lines, wound round the waist of the cap which end in gold acorns, kept apart by the sliders which are turned sideways.

According to Salisbury the sabretache had a blue face which was edged all round with silver lace with a large Royal Cypher in the centre entwined and reversed, with a gold Crown above and the Death's-head and Bones and the Motto label beneath. Forbes' sabretache is certainly blue and is laced all round with silver. The design in the centre is not clear but apparently consists of a pair of lances over which the Cypher and Crown are placed, together with the Death's-head and Bones and Motto label, all in silver. Forbes wears dark blue trousers as worn in Full Dress, laced with silver, and has a Mameluke pattern sword in a steel scabbard and with a gold knot.

The shabraque in Forbes' portrait is blue with white vandykes, laced all round with silver, the design on the fronts consisting of the Crown and Cypher and the design in the hind corners probably

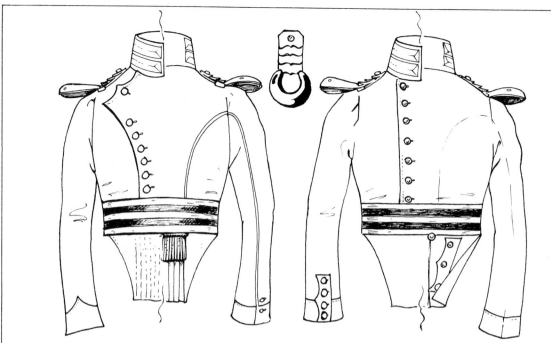

Left *The first blue plastron-fronted coatee. The girdle is white and blue.* **Right** *The red double-breasted coatee of William IV. The girdle is yellow and red.*

the same as described for the sabretache. Over the shabraque is a white sheepskin. The horse has the bridle and breast plate covered with brass scales each decorated with red plumes set in threes in elaborate brass sockets in an oriental design. The single throat plume is also red. On the circular plate in the centre of the breast plate is the Death's-head and this also appears in the centre of the crossed face-piece.

Salisbury also gives an officer in Full Dress, as described above but with dark blue overalls with silver stripes. The Mameluke sword has a steel scabbard and a gold knot. Salisbury has a drawing of a *tschapska* called the 1829 pattern which shows the high-waisted form but has an all-silver figured oak leaf laced band around the waist with a silver band with two blue stripes above and a further wide and narrow silver band below the figured band.

W. Y. Carman has also recorded a portrait of this period. It is a miniature of Lieutenant. W. H. Tonge and is dated about 1827. Mr Carman comments that the late Reverend P. Sumner recorded a number of portraits of this period with the silver aiguelette on the left shoulder but an almost equal number with the aiguelette on the right. Tonge's is on the left. The miniature shows clearly the design of the full dress epaulettes and the design of the aiguelette which differs somewhat from Forbes' type.

The very detailed water colour by Dennis Dighton of a group of officers of the regiment which is in the collection of Her Majesty the Queen in Windsor Castle shows substantially the same uniform. The mounted figure shows, perhaps even more clearly

than the Forbes portrait, the magnificent design of the horse appointments at this period and also the design of the face of the sabretache. The design in the rear pointed corner of the shabraque is the Royal Cypher surmounted by the Crown placed over crossed lances and with the Death's-head and Bones and the Motto beneath.

We are fortunate in having a further portrait, in this case of Lieutenant Henry Charles Witham of the Regiment, dated 1827. This three-quarter length painting provides much intimate detail of the uniform which is not apparent from the broader paintings by the other artists. For example, we can see the design of the lace on the collar and on the cuffs. The cap in this portrait is of particular interest in that it shows clearly the gold cord running up the corners of the top. The chin scales are tied over the front plate. The silver fringed epaulette has a strap embroidered in silver thread on white cloth and the crescent is worked in purl and thread. The 23 short silver bullions are boxed. This portrait gives a very clear picture of the aiguelette and especially the regimental custom of turning the sliders to keep the acorn ends apart. Lieutenant Witham has a small moustache and a goatee beard (See colour plate).

A further drawing by Salisbury of an officer wearing the shell shows this to be a dark blue very short waisted jacket with white collar edged with silver and white pointed cuffs with silver lace edging. The jacket had white cording down the back seams and down the seams of the sleeves. The drawing is back view but no doubt the front was fastened by many small silver buttons, almost touching. The jacket was worn with a Polish style low blue cap with a silver cap band and the square top edged with silver and with a silver cord button with gimp looping and with a central silver cord button and silver and gold tassel. The shell had silver plaited cords on the shoulders. Pale blue pantaloons were worn with this coat with silver stripes down the outside of the legs. A curious ornament appears at the rear of the waist. Two small point-ended tabs appear to support a silver waist belt.

There is another drawing of an officer by Salisbury which shows pale grey overalls with two silver stripes down the outside of each leg and his drawing of a Trooper in marching order indicates the lance cap covered in black oilskin and with white cap lines outside the cover.

The blue jacket has white collar and pointed cuffs but the jacket is buttoned over to show two rows of white metal buttons down the front. The jackets have white turnbacks and white piping up the back seams and sleeves and brass shoulder ornaments with crescents. White gloves. White girdle with two blue stripes. No sabretache. A knob over the lance head. Furled pennon. White waistbelt. Sabre on slings, steel scabbard, brass three bar guard, white sword knot (see colour plate). Plain blue shabraque with the rear corner folded up to show white lining. Rounded fronts and rear. Round blue valise with white piping on the ends and '17L' in white and a white sheepskin.

An officer in marching order from the same source also shows the lance cap in a foul weather black oilskin case. Coat buttoned over. Cap lines over the cover. Silver epaulettes. Grey overalls with two silver stripes down the outside of the legs. No shabraque, black sheepskin.

A Cramer drawing of a Trumpeter gives a white topped *tscahpska* with gold and red cap lines and a red plume. Blue jacket with white collar, cuffs and turnbacks and white buttons. No pouch belt. Mixed white and blue braiding (the design is not clear but seems like linked rectangles) all round the collar and on the edges of the cuffs but not on the lapels. Brass trumpet cords with red and yellow cords. The waist girdle and the band separating the top of the lance cap from the skull part yellow with two red stripes. Black sheepskin, mounted on a grey horse.

An actual specimen of a jacket of this period existed in the collection of the late S. M. Milne and was recorded by P. Sumner. It was dark blue with white collar, pointed cuffs and small turnbacks of white facing cloth. One white loop on each collar front. White metal buttons. The skirts of the jacket deeply pleated between the turnbacks and a white 'waterfall' fringe at the waist.

The Troopers' shabraques were blue, with rounded fronts and hind ends. The fronts were plain but the rear corners had a Silver Crown over a Royal Cypher with crossed lances with red and white pennons behind the Cypher. Below the

Cypher the Death's-head and Bones and Motto label. The shabraques were edged with broad white bands and were lined white. The sheepskins were black.

Officer and Trooper circa 1832

Shortly after he acceded to the throne William IV caused the issue of a General Order which drastically altered the uniform of British cavalry. Henceforth the cavalry uniform was red for all regiments except for the Royal Horse Guards. The 17th Lancers are shown in two oil paintings forming part of the set by Dubois Drahonet in the collection of Her Majesty the Queen at Windsor Castle.

The first painting is of the Lieutenant Colonel the Lord Bingham. Lord Bingham raised the standard of the dress of his regiment to such a level that they soon became known as 'Bingham's Dandies'. One can see from Drahonet's portrait of the Colonel that he exemplified the dandified appearance of the rest of his regiment. His scarlet jacket is cut skin tight with very tight sleeves. The white Prussian collar is very high and the cuffs tiny and served with red cuff flaps with four buttons. The collar, cuffs and the cuff flaps are trimmed with gold. On both shoulders he wears enormous gold bullion epaulettes, the bullions boxed to give the shoulders extra width. The jacket is cut very high in the waist and even allowing for Drahonet's tendency to stylise his figures this gives Lord Bingham a very elegant appearance with very long legs in dark blue overalls, which have double gold stripes down the outside of each leg.

Richard Simpkin produced one of his better water colours of this uniform. The officer is mounted and shows that the sheepskin had now changed to black but that the blue, gold-trimmed shabraque had substantially the same design as described for the late 1820s. The Trooper by Drahonet is shown back view firing a pistol. His *tschapska* has a black skull with a small black leather visor. Brass chin scales suspended from lions' heads and a large brass rayed plate. The back of the cap has a thick leather reinforcement to protect the head from sword cuts. The caned trencher top was reduced in height in 1829 but is still very large. It is still covered in white cloth and the edges and around the top edge are trimmed with yellow cord. The black cocktail feathers are fixed behind the front cockade (which is not visible).

The Trooper wears a tight red jacket with white collar, cuffs, turnbacks and has yellow buttons. The coat was made double-breasted with two rows of brass buttons down the fronts. There were two buttons at the waist level at the rear of the coat but no 'waterfall' fringe. The small skirts had two vertical pocket flaps fastened by two buttons. The Trooper has a brass scaled epaulette on each shoulder and his yellow cap lines are fastened at the back corner of the trencher top by a hook and loop down the back and fasten off round the neck with a slider.

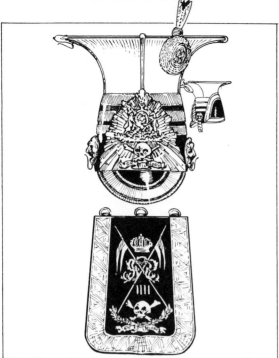

Top *The tschapska of 1829 from an actual specimen, photographed and detailed by W. Y. Carman.* **Above** *The officers' sabretasche. Blue velvet with silver lace border. The crown and lance pennons are in proper colours.*

At this period Troopers of the 17th wore white leather shoulder belts with brass buckles, tips and slides and had black leather pouches without ornaments. The belts had no carbine swivels as lancers carried pistols only besides their lances. The Trooper has a wide yellow worsted girdle with two red stripes which is worn over the jacket. In summer they wore loose white linen trousers and in winter blue-black trousers with yellow stripes. The white leather sword belt was worn under the jacket and had long slings. The 1822-pattern sword had a three-bar brass guard and steel scabbard. The sword knot was white leather. The lance had an ash shaft with a triangular steel head and the pennon was white over red.

A drawing dated 1839 by Michael Angelo Hayes also shows the scarlet coat which lasted until 1840. This shows two officers in the foreground, both wearing the white-topped lance cap with black-green drooping cocktail plumes. They wear white gauntlet gloves. The figures are small and the details are difficult to decipher but it is clear that the shabraques have rounded fronts and hind parts and are blue, edged with gold, and have the Royal Cypher in the front parts and the Crown, Cypher over the lances, Death's-head, Bones and Motto in the rear worked in silver. The sheepskins are black. Both officers have dark blue overalls with gold stripes down the outside of each leg.

In the left foreground of Hayes' plate is the Mounted Band. They also have the lance cap but with red drooping plumes. The jackets are red with white facings and they have white gauntlet gloves. The sheepskins are white and the shabraques blue with gold trimming and devices which seem similar to the officers. The Band are mounted on grey horses. Of particular interest in this painting are the breastplate ornaments of the officers' horses. These are large gilt (?) Death's-heads and Bones.

In 1840 the regiment returned to a blue uniform faced white and a Hayes' plate of this period shows the Band in their new costume. They have white-topped Lance caps with red plumes. Their jackets are blue faced with white and with white buttons and brass shoulder ornaments as one would expect. The overalls are blue with white stripes down the leg and the sheepskins are white. The shabraques have round hind parts, the fronts are not visible. The ornaments on the parts that are visible are similar to those worn during the red coat period. In the foreground of the painting is the Kettle drummer, his drum banners are dark blue, trimmed with silver fringe, and the ornaments are very large Death's-heads and Bones with the Motto label.

P. W. Reynolds has a note of the recorded uniform of a Trooper in the Crimean War. Blue, faced with white, coat buttoned over. Brass shoulder ornaments. Yellow girdle with two red stripes. Grey overalls with two white stripes. White pouch belt. He carries haversack, water canteen and field bag on the saddle. Lance cap covered with black oilskin case, yellow cords outside. Lance pennon furled. Trumpeter ditto with brass trumpet, yellow, blue and red cords. White gauntlets. Grey valise.

In December 1857 the regiment arrived at Bombay dressed in their European clothing of blue jackets, and with overalls strapped with leather. They wore forage caps with fitted visors covered with white and with neck curtains. In D. H. Parry's *Death or Glory Boys* we find that the coats were buttoned to hide the white 'butterfly' lapels and they wore white neck curtains.

In April 1860 the regiments first lost the visors to their caps and later took into use white helmets of leather covered with linen and made by their saddler sergeant who had come to the 17th from the 12th and was much appreciated. Later the same year they adopted khaki with blue piping in the sleeves of shell stable jackets and piping up the back seams. The jackets had white 'stuff' buttons and they wore khaki overalls with two blue stripes and their white helmets had thick muslin puggris. □

Key to colour plates. Top left *Lieutenant Henry Witham, 1827, from the portrait by John Watson Gordon.* **Bottom left** *A trooper in 1829 from the drawing by G. E. Salisbury showing a double breasted coatee.* **Top right** *Lieutenant Colonel Lord Bingham (later Lord Lucan of Crimea fame) from the portrait by Dubois Drahonet, 1832.* **Bottom right** *A trooper from the painting by Dubois Drahonet, 1832.* **Inset left and right** *The shell and Polish-style cap as depicted by Salisbury* **(Paintings by Bryan Fosten).**

THE MONSTERS OF LENINGRAD

Janusz Magnuski and Steven Zaloga on early Soviet heavy tank design

At the outbreak of World War 2, only the armoured force of the Red Army possessed any significant number of heavy tanks. Virtually unknown are the series of heavy tank designs which were the forebears of the famous KV and IS heavy tanks and this article is the first in-depth survey of their development and use.

At the time of the war's outbreak, the most numerous heavy tank type in service with the Red Army was the multi-turreted T-35. The T-35 had been designed at the S. M. Kirov Factory No 185 in Leningrad and was produced in modest numbers from 1934 to 1939. Of the 63 vehicles completed, there were several different series, each with varying armour thicknesses, constructional improvements, armament changes, etc.

The majority of these vehicles were assigned to a single heavy tank brigade headquartered in the Ukraine. One of its battalions was assigned to Kharkov and subsequently to Zhytomir and was commanded from 1937-1939 by Colonel Shtemienko. It was the tanks of this battalion which took part in the famous annual parades in Moscow.

Use of these tanks during the large annual exercises revealed that the tank commanders were handicapped by the lack of centralised fire control system comparable to that used on multi-turreted warships. They did not have any hand sights or target indicators to direct the five turrets during action. Furthermore, the gunners had very narrow fields of vision through the gun telescopes and had a difficult time determining the main target to destroy. Like most tanks of the period, the T-35 had to make a brief halt to aim the guns accurately, and needless to say, the harried driver was hard pressed to stop every time one of the five turrets asked him to do so. Moreover, the more frequent the pauses to aim the guns, the better a target the tank became for enemy gunners.

As a result of Soviet tank crew experiences dur-

ing the Spanish Civil War, it was appreciated that the 15-30 mm of armour used on tanks up until then was inadequate when faced with anti-tank guns in the 20-37 mm range. The impressions garnered from the combat actions in Spain led the Soviet General Staff to direct the Directorate of the Armoured and Mechanised Force (ABTU) to consider the design of new tanks with heavier armour. In the heavy tank class, a new type of vehicle was envisioned to replace the T-35 and was labelled as an 'Anti-tank Gun Destroyer'. Double-layered armour was planned which had to be sufficient to withstand 37-45 mm anti-tank gun fire from any range and 75 mm field gun fire from ranges of about 1,200-1,300 metres.

The design bureau at Leningrad's Factory No 185, directed by N. Barykov, had already designed the first Soviet tank with 60 mm armour during the spring of 1937. This was the T-111 (also known as the T-46-5) and a single prototype was completed in 1938. The Izorski Factory near Leningrad gained very useful experience in the production of heavy armour plate while working on the hull and turret armour for this tank. On the heels of this project, the Barykov design team turned their attention to the new heavy tank requirement, which was designated as the T-100. Concurrently, Leningrad's Kirovski Works design team began their work on a tank based on the same general requirements, which was designated as the SMK (after Sergiey Mironovich Kirov, the former head of the Leningrad Communist Party). In May 1937 the post of design bureau chief fell to Zh. Kotin, a young and extremely talented engineer from the Academy of Mechanisation and Motorisation, who began efforts to reorganise and expand the department.

Compliant with the design specifications, the early proposals for both the SMK and T-100 were multi-turreted, although at an early stage the number of turrets was dropped from five to three with the gun turrets being retained and the machine-gun turrets omitted. Inevitably, the early designs continued the basic conception of the T-35 to some extent. In May 1938 the early designs and models of both tanks were displayed at a special enlarged gathering of the Defence Committee in Moscow. Earlier, while working on their project, both Kotin

---

Key to colour plates. Top *Impression of the SMK heavy tank based on the few available photographs and drawings. Markings appear to have been non-existent or rare at best.* **Bottom** *T-100 based on a photograph of the vehicle as it appeared during the fighting in Finland during 1940* **(Paintings by John Tasker).**

for military modellers

A nice frontal shot of a T-35 during summer manoeuvres in the Ukraine in the late 1930s. The T-35 served as the basis for the subsequent heavy tank designs (all photos copyright © Janusz Magnuski).

and Yermolayev became convinced that the three-turret conception was rather questionable as it greatly increased the vehicle's weight and complicated the design. There was very little time to prepare a detailed proposal before the May 4 meeting, but they demonstrated their wooden models and drawings of the proposals, stressing their new recommendations. Stalin supported Kotin's recommendations and the number of turrets was reduced to two. Various other changes were also ordered including changes from the suspension style as used on the T-35. The question of the production of special steel plate as well as what type of steel to use continued to prove troublesome and the questions were not answered to everyone's satisfaction.

The modified design proposals were submitted at the August 1938 meeting of the Central Committee of the Communist Party; both were accepted, and both factories were instructed to complete prototypes by the end of the following year. At this point, on his own initiative, Kotin decided to approach the heavy tank question in another fashion and began design work on a single-turreted type with heavier armour. Kotin submitted this further proposal and stressed the great advantages of such a design but the project clashed with existing Army proposals. However, the design caught Stalin's eye and he ordered a prototype built as a supplement to the SMK. Final decision on which of the variants would be accepted as the new standard heavy tank of the Soviet Army awaited performance trials.

SMK heavy tank data

Weight — 55 tons; **Crew** — 7 men; **Dimensions** — length: 850 cm, width: 370 cm, height: 320 cm, ground clearance: 50 cm; **Armament** — (main turret): 76.2 mm L-11 tank gun with co-axial 7.62 mm DT machine-gun and 7.62 mm anti-aircraft

machine-gun on roof mount; (subsidiary turret): 45 mm tank gun with co-axial 7.62 mm DT machine-gun; **Armour** — mixed welded, riveted construction of rolled steel plate as well as cast components to a maximum of 60 mm; **Engine** — AM-34 petrol, liquid-cooled engine, four-stroke, 12-cylinder, 800-850 hp; mechanical transmission with clutch and brake steering; **Suspension** — torsion bar, eight road wheels per side with four rubber-rimmed return rollers; drive sprocket to the rear; single-pin metal tracks, 700 mm wide with 630 cm ground contact; **Performance** — maximum speed 36 km/h, 13.7-14.5 hp/ton, 150 km range, trench crossing ability of 350 cm width, 120 cm depth and obstacle clearance of 110 cm.

At the close of 1938, Factory No 185 was in the process of building two prototypes of the T-100. The first of these was completed in May 1939 and at the time was one of the heaviest tanks ever built. It was mainly of welded and bolted construction with the turret and hull front pieces cast. It had a liquid-cooled petrol engine and a fairly complicated suspension with rubber-rimmed road wheels.

The Kirovski Works proceeded with their own projects and at the beginning of 1939 the SMK design work was completed and the plans were sent to the experimental section for final implementation. The Kotin team had completed design work at about the same time on the single-turreted type which was given the designation 'KV' (Kliment Voroshilov, the People's Defence Commissar). Work on the KV proved somewhat simpler since it relied heavily on studies already done for the SMK.

In February 1939, work began on the first SMK prototype and on two KV prototypes. Both were to be equipped with the brand new V-2 diesel built by the Kharkovski Diesel Engine Works No 75. However, the new uprated version of the engine was not ready and it proved necessary to use the AM petrol aircraft engine on a temporary basis. There were still various problems with the armour. The hull and turret armour was ordered from the Izhorski Factory which was already overburdened with contracts from other factories for tanks then in series production. The work on the SMK called for the thickest armour they had ever produced and caused serious delays.

The metallurgists at the Kirovski Works concluded that the solution was to adopt heterogeneous armour rather than homogeneous. These conclusions had already been reached when, in May 1939, they were called to Moscow to a special meeting of the Political Bureau. As a result of the meeting, the Kirovski Works formed a special bureau to find a definite solution to the problem and to lay the groundwork for the adoption of these techniques in all of the Soviet steel works. These matters remained under scrutiny into 1940.

Tank armament for both designs also caused some trouble. The SMK was to be fitted with the L-11 76.2 mm Tank Gun designed at the Kirovski

Works, and a 45 mm gun in the sub-turret. The KV was to be fitted with a new 76.2 mm gun which at the end of 1937 was still under design at Artillery Factory No 92 in Gorki. Designated F-32, this new gun was completed by the middle of 1938 and featured a semi-automatic breech, a longer barrel than the L-11 and a rather modest recoil. Lacking a heavy tank turret for test purposes, it was fitted into a BT light tank turret with the reasoning that if such a combination worked there would be no problems fitting it to a heavy tank turret. As a result, the early KVs were fitted with the L-11 gun.

In August 1939 all three of the vehicles were completed and after a short series of tests on the factory proving grounds, the SMK and one KV were sent by rail to the Soviet tank force proving grounds outside Moscow. On September 1 1939 a demonstration was held there of all of the new designs from tank bureaus around the Soviet Union. Besides the SMK and KV, there were the T-100, the A-20, T-32, and T-29 mediums, modernised T-26, BT-7M, T-30 and T-40 light tanks and a large number of armoured cars. In the subsequent weeks, extensive tests were held, with the KV showing the best results in the heavy tank category.

In December 1939 it was decided to send all of the existing T-100s, SMKs and KVs to Finland to test the vehicles under actual combat conditions

Below *A rear view of a T-35 clearly showing the two rear turrets as well as the commander's radio mast which encircles the turret. This particular vehicle is from the third (modified) production series. The peculiar broken band insignia was a common marking style on the T-35s.* **Bottom** *A model of the second prototype of the SMK as presented to Stalin.*

An artist's reconstruction of the completed SMK.

on the Karelian Isthmus. Shortly afterwards, on December 19, the Defence Committee announced that as a result of the experimental trials held in September, the KV had been officially accepted for service. Simultaneously, the Kirovski Works was instructed to prepare for series production of the type and received a contract for 50 tanks for the following year.

T-100 heavy tank data

Weight — 58 tons; **Crew** — 6-7 men; **Dimensions** — length: 820 cm, width: 345 cm, height: 335 cm, ground clearance: 50 cm; **Armament** — (main turret): 76.2 mm tank gun with co-axial 7.62 mm machine-gun and 7.62 mm anti-aircraft machine-gun on the roof; (subsidiary turret): 45 mm tank gun with co-axial 7.62 mm machine-gun; **Armour** — mixed welded/bolted construction with some cast elements to a maximum of 60-75 mm; **Engine** — 500 hp liquid-cooled petrol engine (with an 850 hp planned); **Suspension** — enclosed spring suspension with eight rubber-rimmed road wheels per side grouped together for bogie assemblies of two wheels; five return rollers, drive sprocket at rear; single-pin metal tracks, 700 mm wide, 580 cm ground contact; **Performance** — 9.0 hp/t, maximum speed of 35 km/h.

On December 17, one SMK and two KVs had been transported by rail to the Russo-Finnish border around Charna Zhechka. From the town, they

A blurry but historically interesting photo of the SMK disabled during the fighting on the Karelian Isthmus in 1940.

A very rare photo of the completed T-100 which was a competitor to the SMK design. Notice the rubber-rimmed road wheels, the boxy 76 mm gun mantlet and the higher rear deck which quickly distinguish it from the SMK.

set off to the build-up point of the 20th Armoured Brigade. Together with one T-100 and another KV, they formed a special heavy tank company under the command of a government commission headed by Major Engineer P. Voroshilov (son of the Minister of Defence after whom the KV was named). Voroshilov also served as the operational field commander of the unit.

The tanks were carefully camouflaged in a pine forest, and shortly afterwards the head of the Armoured Force Directorate, Komkor P. Pavlov, arrived with other officers. The SMK, T-100 and KVs were assigned to one of the most difficult areas of the Finnish fighting. The target area stretched from between Lake Summajarvi and the Sunasuo bog in the direction of the town of Summy. On the left flank the Finnish forces occupied the high ground with several lines of trenches, anti-tank ditches, barbed wire and four rows of anti-tank obstacles.

The following dawn, the Soviet attack began. The early morning haze was first broken by red signal flares followed by heavy artillery salvoes. Entrances were cut through the obstacles by engineers who were followed by infantry in camouflaged white smocks. The crew of the SMK, three of them from the staff of the Kirovski Works, waited for their attack signal from inside the tank. The vehicle commander, Lieutenant Pietin, eventually clambered on board, slammed the hatch shut and shouted through his laryngophone for the driver the start the tank up. The enormous vehicle lurched forward and was soon at the Finnish defence line.

The driver, V. Ignatiev, could see through his narrow view slit as the heavy vehicle brushed aside sizeable pine trees on either side of the narrow path and crushed the flimsy barbed wire entanglements. The SMK crossed one wide anti-tank ditch and crawled over a stone anti-tank obstacle. By this point, small-arms fire could be heard ringing off the armour and this was occasionally drowned out by the ineffective but noisy blast of an artillery round. The SMK was already inside the Finnish defensive line, and after overrunning some more trenches, it destroyed an artillery position and sent its crew running.

In the SMK, the temperature was rising and the cordite fumes were so thick that they burned the eyes and throat. But so far, the tank had passed its

A photo of the rare SU-100 Y which served during the defence of Moscow in 1941.

for military modellers

tests even if it was giving Ignatiev a hard time as driver. From the view slits, the whole hill seemed enveloped in shell bursts. The Russian infantry was taking heavy machine-gun fire, and it was obvious that the Finnish bunkers had to be cleared at once. In the meantime, the main turret traverse had become inoperative and the gun damaged, so Pietin ordered the tank leftward to crush the bunker under its tracks. It took all of Ignatiev's strength to steer the tank and it was quite close to the bunker when suddenly it was rocked by a heavy explosion and engulfed in smoke. When the crew recovered from the blast, they realised they had run over a well camouflaged mine. The explosion had smashed into the bottom of the vehicle, knocking out the electrical installations and the fuel tanks, and as a result the engine could not be re-started. Soon, Finnish infantry swarmed all over the disabled tank but were driven off with machine-gun fire. They attacked several more times but eventually gave up. At that moment, Pietin ordered the tank abandoned and explosive charges set to scuttle it.

The outcome of the experimental employment of the heavy tanks in Finland was the withdrawal of the T-100 and SMK from any serious consideration of mass production in favour of the KV-1 and its artillery tank version, the KV-2. From this chassis, the Kirovski Works proceeded with further design studies for one prototype example of a new improved vehicle, designated the SMK-2, which differed markedly from the SMK.

By this time, the Red Army had already broken through the first layer of Finnish screening defences and now faced the main defensive barrier, the Mannerheim Line. This line had both wooden and concrete bunkers which could withstand direct large calibre artillery hits. The commander of the Soviet 7th Army, K. Miereckov, wrote, 'For five days we were preparing for our latest attack, but without any success. It was again apparent that we lacked the experience and means to overcome these formidable strongpoints. Existing tanks simply did not have large enough guns to destroy these defences by themselves. The best we could do was to cover their firing ports with the tank hulls.'

In these circumstances, a gun of 152-203 mm was needed, but it was not a simple matter to haul so large a gun up to forward positions to deal with bunkers and so a heavy self-propelled gun provided the obvious solution. In February 1940, the KV-2 was first tested. Independently from this project, the Kirovski Works was preparing another heavy self-propelled gun designated SU-212 (Obiekt 212) which could be fitted with either the 152 mm Br-2 gun or the 203 mm B-4 howitzer. This was based on a lengthened KV hull but work was interrupted by the German invasion in June 1941.

At the same time, Factory No 185 was rebuilding one of the T-100 prototypes as a self-propelled gun. Both turrets were removed and replaced by a large fixed casemate housing a 130 mm B-13 naval gun as used on contemporary Soviet destroyers. Work on the design was not completed until after the war with Finland and it saw no action there. In the summer of 1940, it was sent to the Odessa Military District for firing trials against both land and naval targets. At first it was designated as the T-100 U Heavy Tank (U – *Uluchshonniy* = Improved) but it was subsequently redesignated as the SU-100 Y. At the time of the war, the SU-100 Y was transported to the Moscow Military District where it took part in the defence of Moscow in the autumn of 1941.

SU-100 Y heavy self-propelled gun data

Weight — 60 tons; **Crew** — 6 men; **Dimensions** — overall length: 1,095 cm, hull length: 810 cm, width: 345 cm, height: 355 cm; **Armament** — 130 mm B-13 gun, shell weight 33 kg, initial muzzle velocity 850 m/s; **Armour** — mixed welded/bolted to 60 mm; **Engine** — M-17 petrol V-12, 500 hp four-stroke, subsequently another type of water-cooled engine of 850 hp; **Performance** — maximum speed of 35 km/h.

In 1940, shortly after the beginning of KV-1 and KV-2 series production, the design bureau of the Kirovski Works began studies of a related heavy tank design which was even further uparmoured and upgunned and which was intended for series production in 1941. The project was called KV-3 at the factory and work proceeded on two versions, the Model 220 (Obiekt 220) and Model 222 (Obiekt 222). The Model 220 was virtually a new tank with only a few major elements from the KV-1 and was planned to have a new gun, engine and transmission, while the Model 222 was a modernised KV-1 with a number of improvements such as thicker armour, a commander's cupola and so on. The KV-3 project was headed by Zh. Kotin.

Consideration was also given to a proposed KV-4 (100 tons) and KV-5 (150 tons) which were based on the KV-3 design work. In comparison to the KV-1, the new KV-3 had a lengthened hull with an extra roadwheel on each side and a larger turret which was basically a cut-down KV-2 turret. A planetary transmission was planned for the tank which was nearing completion, but the first prototype was fitted with a strengthened unit from a KV-2. It was supposed to be armed with the new long-barrelled F-39 gun being designed by V. Grabin's team at Artillery Factory No 92 in Gorki. The actual design work was complete at the beginning of 1941 when unforeseen difficulties cropped up which slowed its completion.

B. Vannikov, at the time the People's Armament Commissar, recalls: 'Several months before the war's outbreak, the People's Armament Commissariat came to experience a severe test. The head of the Central Directorate Artillery, Marshal I. Kulik, informed us that in light of the latest intelligence information, Germany was increasing the tempo of equipping its Panzerwaffe with tanks known to be uparmoured to the point that they would render our artillery in the 45 mm - 76.2 mm range ineffective. For this reason, our own tanks would have to be armed with guns of 100 mm or more. In relation to this arose the problem of completely halting production of 45 mm and 76.2 mm guns and redirecting all efforts to the production of a 107 mm gun, primarily the tank variant.'

After discussion with Stalin and others, Kulik's views prevailed and 45 mm and 76 mm gun production was halted for all services. On April 5 1941, V. Grabin was ordered to begin design work on a 107 mm gun for the Leningrad heavy tank project, in the shortest time possible. An extremely tight schedule was worked out and in spite of the complexity of the design, involving some 387 major components, by May 28 1941 the prototype was ready. The gun was designated ZIS-6 and prepared and shipped to the Kirovski Works in Leningrad. There it was test fired and certain improvements were recommended. On July 15, following the war's outbreak, the gun was prepared for mounting on

Above right *A very interesting view of the rear of the SU-100 Y. This vehicle was originally known as the T-100 U.* **Right** *A series production KV-1 from the original production batch in 1939-40.*

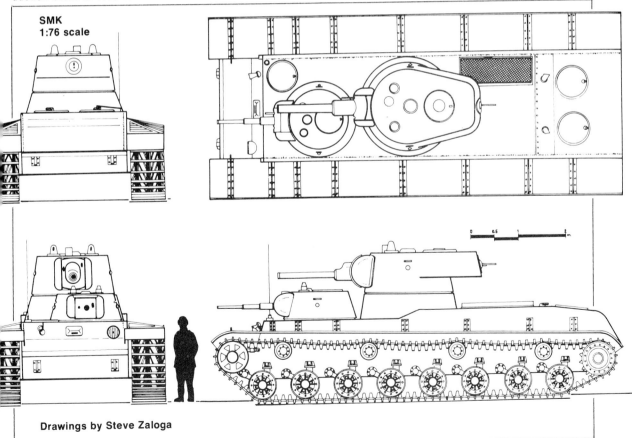

SMK
1:76 scale

Drawings by Steve Zaloga

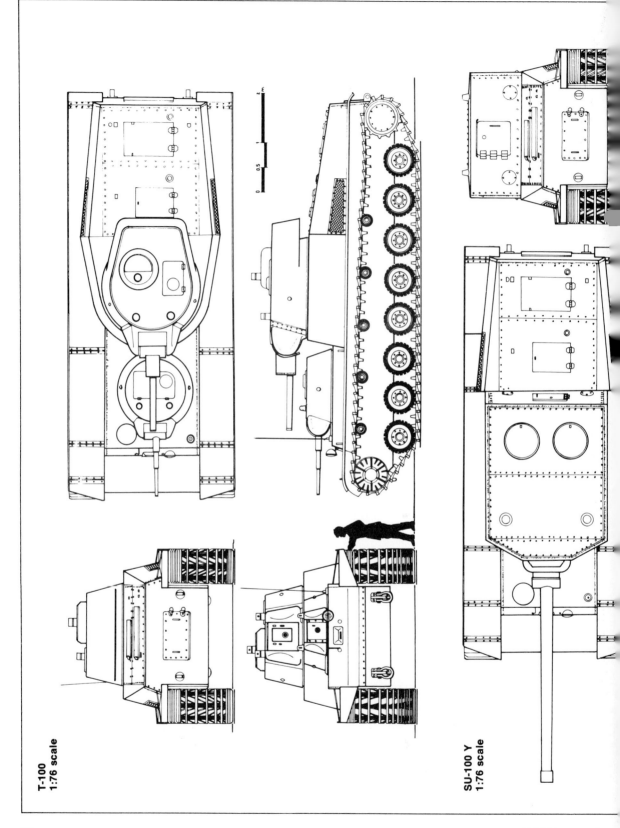

T-100
1:76 scale

SU-100 Y
1:76 scale

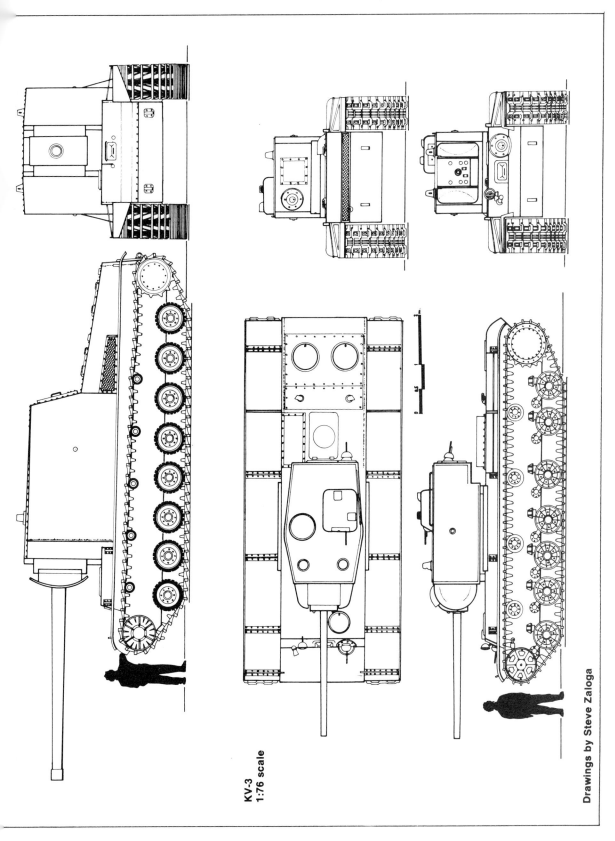

KV-3
1:76 scale

Drawings by Steve Zaloga

Above left *A photo of the Model 222 (KV-3) which was essentially a KV-1 with increased armour, a commander's cupola and other features, many of which were never incorporated on subsequent production types.* **Above** *A KV-2 from the initial production batch.* **Below left** *The prototype for the KV-3 (Model 222) which was supposed to replace the KV-1 and become the standard heavy tank of the Red Army in the 1940s. Note the lengthened hull and new turret with 85 mm gun.*

the KV-3, but due to the military situation, this was not completed. Series production was not initiated and only a few prototype examples were built.

Even prior to this, there had been problems with the engine as the usual V-2 powerplant proved insufficient for so heavy a chassis. At the end of 1940, the Kirovski Works was preparing for production a special version of the liquid-cooled M-40 diesel engine. Two new groups were assigned to this project and it was nearing completion in the spring of 1941. Changes and improvements were scheduled, and the version of the M-40 developed for the KV-3 was designated as the V-2PUN. Independent of this, at the end of 1940, the Kharkov Diesel Engine Works had developed another engine on the basis of an existing aircraft type, the V-2SN, which also was more powerful than the V-2. Improvements took time but in June 1941 a prototype was completed and sent to Leningrad for mounting in the KV-3 hull.

In spite of these difficulties, the first two prototypes were finished at the beginning of 1941. In May 1941 field tests without armament were conducted and it was officially accepted for quantity production, as a standard tank of the Red Army. This was to take place at the Chelyabinsk Tractor Factory (ChTZ) where preparations had already been begun. ChTZ had already received a portion of the technical documentation and one of the prototypes prior to the outbreak of war. However, the

war forced a reconsideration of whether it was best to introduce a new tank type with a complicated gun, new engine and transmission and other features which would probably slow down production of other types, and as a result, the plans were withdrawn.

The other KV-3 tanks in Leningrad were provisionally armed with either 85 mm or 100 mm naval guns and took part in the city's defence. One of these tanks, driven by V. Ignatiev, defended the bridge near the Krashnievski cemetery, covering the approaches to the Kirovski Works along the Peterhofski route. The fate of the other vehicles is not known.

KV-3 (Model 220) heavy tank data

Weight — 63 tons; **Crew** — 5-6 men; **Dimensions** — overall length: 840 cm, hull length: 735 cm, width: 325 cm, height: 310 cm, ground clearance: 50 cm; **Armament** — (1st variant): 85 mm F-39 tank gun with automatic breech and loader, co-axial 7.62 mm DT, 7.62 mm DT in sub-turret, 7.62 mm DT at turret rear and in hull; (2nd variant): 107 mm ZiS-6 tank gun with automatic breech and loader; **Armour** — welded with some castings to 100 mm; **Engine** — 850 hp V-2PUN, four-stroke, 12-cylinder, liquid-cooled diesel; **Transmission** — multiple disc clutch, five forward and one reverse gear with strap brakes; clutch and brake steering; **Suspension** — seven steel-rimmed roadwheels per side on torsion bars with externally mounted dampers, rear-mounted drive sprocket and four return rollers; metal tracks, single-pin type 700 mm wide, 2,620 mm between the centres of both tracks; **Performance** — 13.6 km/t, maximum speed of 33-35 km/h. □

FORWARD COMMAND POST

Terry Wise outlines some simple kit conversions for dioramas or wargames

The Forward Command Post set is a gold mine for the wargaming-modeller, with its oil drums, ammo boxes, tools, etc, but our primary concern here will be the building itself and its base. Base and building make up into an attractive diorama, garnished with as many of the accessories as you fancy, but their active use in a wargame is limited by accessibility to the nooks and crannies for figures employed in the actual fighting rather than as static HQ figures for show only. The various items vac-formed into the base also limit the use of the post to World Wars 1 and 2, and therefore the aim of this article is to produce buildings which can be used for the 18th and 19th Centuries without the base, or for the 20th Century with or without the base.

First take two kits, setting aside for the moment all the accessories and the bases. From the building parts we shall now make two ruined houses, different to those shown in the kit instructions, with the opportunity of using these 'new' buildings individually or together as one larger, L-shaped building.

First building completed, with separate strongpoint taken from the original base. Note 'whitewash' on part of outer wall: this was Polyfilla smeared over a section of wall where rock marking was incomplete. Note also the small corner section, described at the end of the second building construction.

1st Building

The main disadvantage (for the wargamer) of the kit as it stands is the difficulty in inserting figures into the inner room of the ruin, both the roof and upper floor making handling of figures in this area difficult. Therefore, in this first building we will do away with the roof so that figures may be placed more easily in the inner room and behind the chimney breast wall — the main field of fire in the original kit being this end of the ruin.

One word of warning before you start: care should be taken during assembly to ensure all corners are exact right angles, otherwise problems will occur when placing the buildings on their bases.

Cement Part 1 to Part 2 after removing the tabs from inside the chimney stack, so the stack is clear when viewed from above. Cement Part 4 to Part 2, and Part 5 to Part 4 as per the kit instructions. Take the second Part 4 and cut off the end section, cutting down a line between the holes designed to receive Part 5. Chamfer this edge and remove the chamfer from the opposite end. Cement the newly chamfered end to the other side of the chimney breast (where Part 8 goes in the kit).

Take the second Part 5, remove the studs, and cement this to your modified Part 4 to form a second side wall slightly longer than the first. Cement a Part 7, with chamfered edge removed, on the

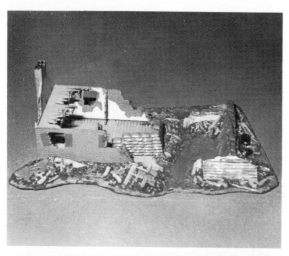

Top *First building from the other side and with a Parts 9-10 sandbag unit in position. The extra pile of rubble in the interior, to help clip the building in position, can be seen at the extreme end of the far wall.* Above *Second building completed. The far wall has been lifted slightly to show where the rubble on the 'floor' has been cut to receive it.* Below *Other side of second building. The added pile of rubble is at the end of the far wall.*

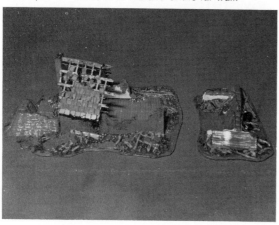

interior of the longest side wall, where Parts 4 and 5 are joined: this should line up with the cross wall from the other side, creating an inner room with the doorway destroyed. I trimmed the top of Part 7 to make what I thought was a more realistic shape.

Two Part 3s can be used either as designed, ie, pinned into the top edges of the Part 5s, which looks a bit odd and makes access difficult again; or you can remove the studs and cement the floor sections side by side across Part 2. In this case remove the stud from Part 2 and shorten one Part 3 by two planks.

2nd Building

Here we keep the roof but omit the upper floor to allow easier handling of figures in the interior.

Assemble Parts 1 and 2 as before but enlarge the slot at the top of Part 2 to receive the ends of two ridge planks. Take a Part 8, cut off short at the point where the wall is broken down to its lowest level, and cement the longer section to Part 2 as per the kit instructions. Take the second Part 8 and cement it to the other edge of Part 2 to form a second side wall, with the fully stone-marked face forming the outer surface of the wall. To the other end of this wall cement at right angles the remnant left from Part 4 when making the first building.

Cement the two Part 6s together along the ridge plank. Make the outer ends of the ridge planks 'broken' and trim the other ends to fit into the slot in Part 2 without protruding into the stack. Cement this roof to Part 2 where it touches: at the slot in the stack; along the end wall on the right; and at the corners where the side walls join the end wall. Cut off any rafters protruding beyond the end wall. You will note the roof is now sloping down towards the centre of the building, as if about to collapse.

Two other oddments remain, a Part 7 and an oddment from a Part 8. Cement these together at right angles, after reducing to the same height where they touch, to form an odd corner which can be used with either building, on or off their bases.

The bases

The bases can also be modified slightly, and need a little work in any case as the shell holes prevent them sitting flush on a table top, and the road, curb and drain details are not appropriate to wargaming, since they will not normally link up with similarly modelled roadways.

The base for the first building may be cut as shown in the photos. Here the road and drain have been totally cut away, the curb disguised with Plasticine, and the sandbagged end detached. The shell hole was cut from underneath so that it was flush with the rest of the base. This abbreviated base was then cemented to strong card, after weighting the base with Plasticine pushed into the raised parts; any gaps caused by the cutting were plugged with Plasticine. To ensure the building clipped firmly on

A third kit made up as instructions except the roof is on the opposite side to give better access to the interior; Part 7 and a small piece of scrap have been added round the upper floor to provide some cover; and the base has been trimmed to remove road, drain and gutter details. The corner from a Part 7 and an oddment of Part 8 is also used.

to the base, an extra pile of rubble was placed in the corner nearest the shell hole. This rubble was made of epoxy resin covered with body putty with a piece of matchstick protruding. The off-cut of sandbags was similarly trimmed, weighted and cemented to card, and forms a useful little strongpoint in built-up areas.

The base for the second building was treated in the same manner, but this time the corrugated iron end was cut off to form an independent strongpoint. Again an extra pile of rubble was made to hold the building firmly on its base, this time just beside the oil drum. The extra long wall, and the corner at its end, means that on the opposite side the walls cannot fit into the base because of vac-formed rubble. This is turned to advantage by cutting slots in the rubble to receive the walls, thus holding the building even more securely.

Parts 9-10 of the kits can be filled with Plasticine, scored to represent sandbags, and also used as independent strongpoints or with the buildings.

Painting

The colours suggested in the kit can be followed, particularly the dry-brushing with black to simulate fire or explosive marks. I used my own red/yellow mix for a clay tile colour; a red/brown shade on the stonework to represent sandstone, rubbed over with my fingers when the paint was dry; a yellowish shade on the woodwork for light oak; and off-white as 'whitewash' on the surviving plaster on the interior walls. The bases were treated with an overall black wash, followed by a brown one, to highlight all the crevices and objects, these objects then being painted in their various colours — plaster, tiles, stone — with the sandbags in khaki drill and oil drums and corrugated iron in gunmetal streaked with rust and silver.

There will be a considerable number of useful items remaining in your boxes. The corrugated iron is invaluable in all post-1900 building work, and the tables and trestle tops can be used as planking. All the boxes and drums go straight into my 'supply depot' for issue later as food, ammo and fuel. The little ammo boxes (54-56) can have the lid cut off and stuck on top to increase the number of these supply items.

The transmitter is used as such in HQ vehicles or can double as a generator in a mobile workshop. The cable reels can be used either with a pair of signallers laying telephone wires, or in the rear of a wire-laying signals vehicle, or as winch drums on engineer vehicles. The bicycles and tools are useful additions for AFV and soft-skin models, as are some of the boxes. The signposts have a limited use but 72 and 74, if cut down a little, can be used for minefield notices. The cable (57-60) is ideal on the fronts of soft-skins, such as the Matador, while the barriers (65-70) can also be used as three-legged anti-tank 'Czech hedgehogs' or beach obstacles, making the third leg for each end piece from the central pole section. □

sFH 18 GUN DETACHMENT

Roy Dilley combines Airfix figures with a metal gun kit to build an imposing diorama

Among the more interesting and expressive military groups are those formed by artillery detachments whilst serving their guns. They can vary from the studied formality of training groups, each 'number' in drill-book pose and placing, to the purposeful urgency of campaign situations, not forgetting the colourful precision of saluting detachments in all the glory of full-dress. There is a definite factor in the relationship of men to equipments that makes the gun detachment a popular subject for modelling, whatever the period to be depicted.

Strangely enough, compared with other 'teeth' arms, cavalry and infantry, artillery personnel have not figured over-prominently in the ranges produced by most commercial manufacturers, whether of toy, kit, or connoisseur types; they are generally included, but not in any great variety, even to serve those artillery pieces that are available in model form. It is therefore very much up to the modeller himself to make his own gun detachments if anything is required other than that which the limited commercial items can supply.

Fortunately, particularly for modellers interested in World War 2, the Airfix Multipose range of figures can provide considerable scope for custommade artillerymen with a minimum of actual con-

version, just by using some imagination in the selection and putting together of parts from different sets. All are designed very carefully to the same scale, and the components are almost completely interchangeable. Their comparatively low cost, much less than £1 Sterling for six figures and a whole stack of equipment and weapons, the ease with which they can be worked, and the really excellent design in terms of anatomy and reliable uniform detail, make them one of the most useful and exciting ranges available to modellers at the present time.

The incentive for the construction exercise described in this article came with the issue by Hinchliffe Models of their terrific 1:32 scale replica of the World War 2 period German 15 cm field howitzer, known as the sFH 18. This magnificent artillery piece, most impressive when assembled and painted, just cried out for presentation in an action situation, complete with detachment of gunners. Alas, no suitable models of German artillerymen of this period can be obtained at less than 'connoisseur' prices, so far as is known; but, not to despair! Multipose to the rescue! Parts from a couple of boxes of German Infantry and Afrika Korps, the facilities offered by a well-stocked spares box, a

Left *The Unterwachmeister (right) with his hands over his ears, and the Kanonier with rammer.* **Centre** *The Oberleutnant.* **Right** *The Obergefreiter captured in the moment of pulling the lanyard* (all photos by Don Disley).

little plastic sheet and rod, plus some time spent in 'doodling' and assembly, was all that was necessary to represent a detachment serving in north west Europe, Italy, or on the Eastern Front.

The attitudes assumed by the figures are consistent with the actions of a detachment in the instant of their gun firing, but it will be appreciated by readers that, such is the flexibility of the basic components, practically any figure position can be achieved with, at most, only the expenditure of a little time and trouble in addition to exercise of the imagination. Provided the anatomical principles of shape, balance and proportion are observed, there is no reason why even an inexperienced modeller cannot turn out authentic figures in attitudes uniquely of his own wishes. Unless one is, or has been, a gunner, it is probably desirable to use drill-books and/or photographs of gun detachments to avoid perpetrating too many gross errors of placement and function in the members of a model detachment.

As for the gun, it presents no real problems, it being necessary only to follow the maker's assembly and painting instructions carefully and thoroughly, ensuring that any flash or mould seams are removed from all the parts before they are fixed together.

Scenic settings can be as simple or complex as inclination may dictate or expertise will permit, but, again, it is better not to let the background overpower the main subject. In particular, moderation should be the watchword in the use of 'clutter' and accessories, using only what is desirable to give a convincing impression of location without it being overdone.

Having made these general points, it is possible to examine more specifically how the gun 'numbers' in the detachment illustrated were made. In each case, the English nomenclature has been used to describe ranks, with the correct German titles following in brackets.

Lieutenant (Oberleutnant)

This raised no difficulties at all, being made up generally as described for Figure 'B' in the Airfix assembly sheet for the German Infantry set, but with a change of head (Part 1). The attitude of the right arm was varied from the example, the pistol has been omitted from the left hand, and a binocular case, made by trimming a canteen (Part 53) was fitted to the front of the belt. Incidentally, no respirator cases (Parts 80-85) have been used on any of the figures in this group.

Sergeant (Unterwachtmeister)

Modelled as if turning away from the gun and shielding his ears from its explosion, the Sergeant was assembled from Parts 27 and 30, body and legs, and head (Part 6) with mouth open, all from the German Infantry set, surmounted by a side-cap (Part 61), left over from the British 8th Army kit, modified to make the German *feldmütze*. The arms, (Parts 23 and 24) were adjusted at elbows and wrists, a process of trial and error being used to locate the hands, cupped over the ears, and obtain the necessary bending at the elbows. This was made easier by severing the arms completely at elbows and wrists, trial fitting them with a minimum of adhesive, paring away surfaces until the right conformation was obtained, then securing with more adhesive, filling in any gaps with liquid plastic and finally sanding down. Folds in the cloth were properly indicated by gentle strokes of a mouse-tail file, and a pistol holster (Part 76) was attached to the left hip.

Bombardier (Obergefreiter)

The figure is depicted in the act of jerking the firing lanyard of the howitzer, and incorporated were body (Part 22), legs (Part 25), arms (Parts 4 left, and 23 right, respectively), and head (Part 21) from the German Infantry kit. The peaked cap, mod-

*Left The Gefreiter setting a shell fuze. **Centre** The Oberkanonier carrying a cartridge case. **Right** The two Kanoniers carrying a round in its shell cradle.*

ified to the 1943 pattern *einheitsmütze,* is a spare part from an Afrika Korps sprue. Left and right rifle ammunition pouches and a scabbarded bayonet on the left hip were also added to the figure, which had the left arm bent, by the same technique as for the Sergeant, across the front of the body, and the hand clenched around a lanyard, made from fine nylon thread. Here again, a little time spent in trial assembly enabled a convincing attitude to be achieved before cementing the parts firmly together, filling and sanding where necessary.

Lance-Bombardier (Gefreiter)

For this kneeling figure, representing the fuze-setter in the detachment, the German Infantry legs (Part 20) were used, with a body (Part 27), head (Part 1) and pistol holster (Part 49) from the Afrika Korps set. The right knee was turned outwards to give more stability, and the head was bent forward on the neck so that the face pointed downwards. Both arms (Parts 28 and 29) were taken from the Infantry kit and fitted to the figure, with a metal shell, supplied with the gun, and a scratch-built spanner gripped in the right hand. Another 8th Army side-cap provided the head-dress, and the holstered pistol was fixed to the left side of the belt. Fuzes were actually set by means of a machine, the setter is checking that the operation has been carried out properly.

Senior Gunner (Oberkanonier)

Made from legs (Part 30) and head (Part 11) from the Infantry set, assembled with Afrika Korps' body (Part 22) and arms (Parts 18 and 19) from the 8th Army kit, this figure is carrying the cartridge-case forward for the next round to be fired. The left arm needed some adjustment to grip the top of the case, but the parts went easily together and made a nicely balanced model. Both peaked cap and pistol holster at left hip were also taken from the Afrika Korps kit.

Gunner (Kanonier)

The same main components as for the Bombardier were used for this figure with the rammer, assembled in a slightly different attitude, and with a side-cap and pistol holster replacing the peaked cap and bayonet. A length of 1 mm plastic rod with a 'head' cut from a piece of sprue made the rammer itself.

Gunner (Kanonier)

As one of a pair of figures shown carrying forward a round in a shell-cradle, this piece was worked on in conjunction with the next conversion, so that balance and cohesion could be maintained. This model is on the right side of the pair facing forwards, and his head was turned inwards towards the shell. The components were marching legs (Part 5) and left arm (Part 4) from the Infantry kit, with body (Part 2) and head (Part 11) from the Afrika Korps, whilst the straight right arm is modified from one obtained from the spares box, coming originally from the Airfix Collectors' Series 1815 Guardsman. In assembly, the body was bowed forward as if under the shell's weight, and the arms were drawn in to the body, some paring away of plastic at the shoulders being required to get the right positioning. The body was also twisted a little to the left at the waist, and the left ankle was turned so that the foot pointed forward. All this is difficult to describe, but comes together naturally enough with a careful 'dry run'. Side-cap, rifle ammunition pouches and scabbarded bayonet complete the piece.

Gunner (Kanonier)

Similar components were used for this model as for the previous conversion, but in assembly the body was turned to the right, both arms were drawn more in front of the torso, and the head was brought to look more in the direction of travel. A pistol holster was used instead of ammunition pouches and bayonet.

For the shell-cradle, carried between the two men, handles were bent from plastic rod, joined by two straight lengths over which was cemented a plastic sheet platform curved to the shape of one of the shells supplied in the gun kit.

All painting was done in a mixture of enamels and artists' oil colours, using uniform data obtained from readily available sources of references such as Martin Windrow's *World War 2 Combat Uniforms and Insignia* (PSL, 1977).

It is emphasised that an exercise of this kind becomes very much a reflection of the individual modeller's preferences, and the great advantage of working with Multipose components is that almost anything in the way of animation can be achieved without undue difficulty. □

STUKAS IN THE SUN
BOFORS 40mm
MIDD

THE ASSAULT ON MALBORGETTO BLOCKHOUSE

Otto von Pivka describes a Napoleonic siege
which would make an unusual wargame

In the early stages of the 1809 campaign Erzherzog Johann, commander of the Austrian force in Italy, defeated his Franco-Italian adversaries at the battle of Sacile on April 16 and seemed poised to sweep them down the Italian peninsula and into the sea. The sudden news which then reached him of the Austrian defeat at Regensburg (Ratisbon) in Bavaria and the subsequent withdrawal of the main Austrian army towards Vienna stopped his advance, however, and caused him to decide to withdraw northwards through the Alps so as to concentrate his army with that of the Kaiser's to defend the capital. His victorious men were then faced with the depressing and difficult task of retreating in the face of a beaten enemy up through the tortuous, rocky defiles from Udine to Villach.

While the overall aim of this move was a withdrawal, the Austrians had selected two blocking positions in the mountains which they had half

prepared for defence and at which they intended to delay their pursuers for some time. The smaller, eastern one of these was a blockhouse and rampart complex at Predil (on the road from Tarvis south to Flitsch on the Isonzo River) and the larger was near the village of Malborgetto on the Fella River west of Tarvis. Hurried attempts were made to complete these positions and to garrison them and equip them with supplies and artillery and, in fact, both forts were in some state of defence by the time the Franco-Italians under Prince Eugene came up to them.

We shall study the conduct of the defence of Malborgetto which provides an interesting little wargame scenario, unusual in that the terrain is extremely mountainous thus offering little room for manoeuvre or deployment (artillery and cavalry were entirely restricted to the roads), limited fields of fire for artillery and the opportunity for a small

Key to colour plates These figures, painted by Michael Stringer from sketches prepared by the author, themselves based on eye-witness accounts from this theatre of operations in 1809, differ in many respects from the uniform regulations of the time. The French Line infantry Lieutenant on the left wears standard dark blue coat with long tails, white lapels and turnbacks piped red, dark blue cuff flaps, etc, but has the red, piped white, collar of a Light infantryman while his shako bears a lozenge-shaped front plate instead of a lenticular one. His epaulettes are also missing the red stripe of his rank. The sapper alongside him is even more perplexing, particularly in respect of the grenade badge on his shako, which should be a bearskin anyway! Similarly, although the Light infantry Corporal third from left is basically accoutred as a Chasseur, his collar should be piped white not green and he should have two red bars of rank on orange backings, not a single bar of silver on red (the distinction of a Marechal des Logis). Moreover, the eagle plate on his shako is white metal not brass, while red over green plumes were only worn by Imperial Guard units. One is only left to speculate on these strange departures from

the rules.

The Austrian figures present fewer problems. The artillery Kanonier in the centre wears the standard plain black bicorn with gold button and loop and black over yellow plume, deer brown tunic with red collar, cuffs, turnbacks, skirt tail and shoulder strap piping, white breeches and boots. The young drummer beside him and the figure on the far right are both from the Oguliner Grenz-Infanterie-Regiment. They wear the normal black felt shakos with black within yellow pompoms, brass loops and black within yellow cockades; tobacco brown tunics with orange-yellow collars, cuffs, turnbacks, shoulder strap and skirt tail piping; white 'bear's claws' tasselled lace decorations to cuffs; sky blue breeches with black and yellow side seams and thigh knots; black belts and pouches and brown calfskin packs. The drummer wears yellow and white swallows' nests and carries a brass drum with yellow and black bands. The penultimate figure on the right is an officer of engineers in black bicorn with dark green plume; pike grey coat, green collar, cuffs and turnbacks; yellow and black wool sash; white breeches.

for military modellers

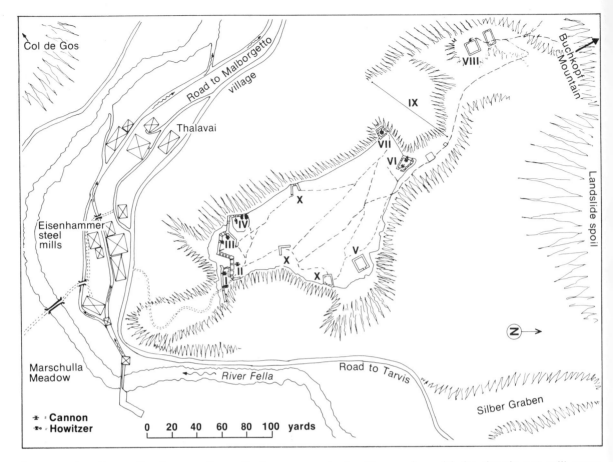

force to bar the path of many times their own number. It would make an ideal 'Brigade' game as suggested elsewhere here by Paddy Griffiths.

General situation May 15 1809

Erzherzog Johann had his headquarters in Villach with Feldmarschalllieutenant (FML) Frimont's division in Arnoldstein and FML Albert Gyulai's division (3,000 men) forward at Saifnitz as rearguard. Predil and Malborgetto were garrisoned and armed. Prince Eugene's men were in Malborgetto village, to the north and south of Predil and were in the Dogna Valley having been ambushed at Wolfsbach at 2 am that day and pushed back from their attempt to outflank Malborgetto. The Austrians had destroyed all the many bridges along the Fella valley road but had left those on other routes intact.

The Malborgetto blockhouse site

Nature had provided nearly the perfect barrier at this point about 500 metres east of the little village of Malborgetto. The deep, ragged trench in which the Fella river flowed was almost closed by an abrupt, flat-topped, steep-sided spur of land which jutted from the north side of the valley, crushing the river and the road which followed it against the southern wall in a gap only 350 paces wide. This natural defile was further restricted by the Thalavai

steel mill complex with its deeply cut mill races which huddled in the shadows at the southern tip of the outcrop.

The top of the outcrop had been rimmed with a low stone wall and covered way and in the enclosure a number of isolated defence works had been built (see plan B). These works extended from south to north as follows.

From the Malborgetto-Tarvis road a track led up the spur and into the Outwork (I), about 12 metres above the valley floor, and on up through the 'Retour' Battery (II) (another seven metres up) which was pierced for artillery and covered the road. West of this was the 'Wiesen' or Meadow Battery (III) whose field of fire played more towards Malborgetto, and west again was the 'Malborgetto' battery (IV) from which artillery could bombard the village itself as well as the road. Both these batteries were cut five metres down into the rock and covered with a bombproof roof of logs and earth. North of this was a gun position (X), the 'Schachtel' Blockhouse (VII) which covered the other blockhouse at the northern tip of the enclosed area and the 'Zwischen' or Intermediate Battery (VI) also cut into the rock and having a bombproof roof. Along the eastern side of the barrier was the 'Ungarisches' or Hungarian Blockhouse (V) 10 x 8 metres, on the highest point of the plateau and

The storming of the Malborgetto outwork.

another two gun positions (X, X). North of the enclosed spur was a cable lift (IX) used to bring up supplies and above this the 'Deutsches' or German Blockhouse (VIII) ten metres square, which lay outside the perimeter of the fort. North of this was a pallisaded trench. Fire from the Schachtel could cover the German Blockhouse.

The spur then ran up towards the Buchkopf mountain with landslide scree to the east. Both blockhouses (Hungarian and German) were of logs on a stone base, two stories high with an open platform with breastwork on top. The entrances were closed with drawbridges and portcullises.

South of the Fella River the valley wall rose again to the Col de Gos, a good position for the enemy to overlook the barrier. The width of the valley could be covered by a musket shot. There was much dead ground in all approaches to the fort and this allowed an enemy assault to find many spots to shelter from the defenders' fire.

The artillery of the fort was distributed as follows: Outwork — two 3 pdr cannon; 'Retour' — one 3 pdr cannon; 'Wiesen' — two 3 pdr cannon; 'Malborgetto' — one 6 pdr, one 3 pdr cannon and one 7 pdr howitzer; 'Zwischen' — two 12 pdr cannon; 'Schachtel' — one 6 pdr cannon. Ammunition stocks were: 140 rounds of ball and ten of grape for each 12 pdr; 280 ball and 32 grape for each 6 pdr;

and 240 ball and 48 grape for each 3 pdr. The howitzer had 80 shells and 20 'Rolling Bombs' were stockpiled at the Outwork. There were also 36,000 infantry cartridges.

The garrison consisted of: the commander — a Captain of engineers; two Captains, two First Lieutenants, one Second Lieutenant, two Ensigns, 200 Fusiliers and 50 Sharpshooters (including the necessary non-commissioned officers) from the Oguliner Grenz-Infanterie-Regiment; one Oberfeuerwerker and 23 gunners for the artillery; plus 13 men (including two bakers) from the engineers; a total of 294 officers and men.

The Franco-Italians occupied Malborgetto on May 15 and stayed there until dawn the next day when they advanced along the road to assault the blockhouse complex and were quickly driven back by artillery and small-arms fire with heavy loss. They then climbed up the southern valley wall (the Col de Gos) but, harassed by fire from the Austrians, could only do so as individuals or in very small groups. Later on the 16th, the Franco-Italians occupied the slopes of the Buchkopf mountain and poured small-arms fire down into the blockhouse complex so that the garrison could not move outside the buildings or the communication trench

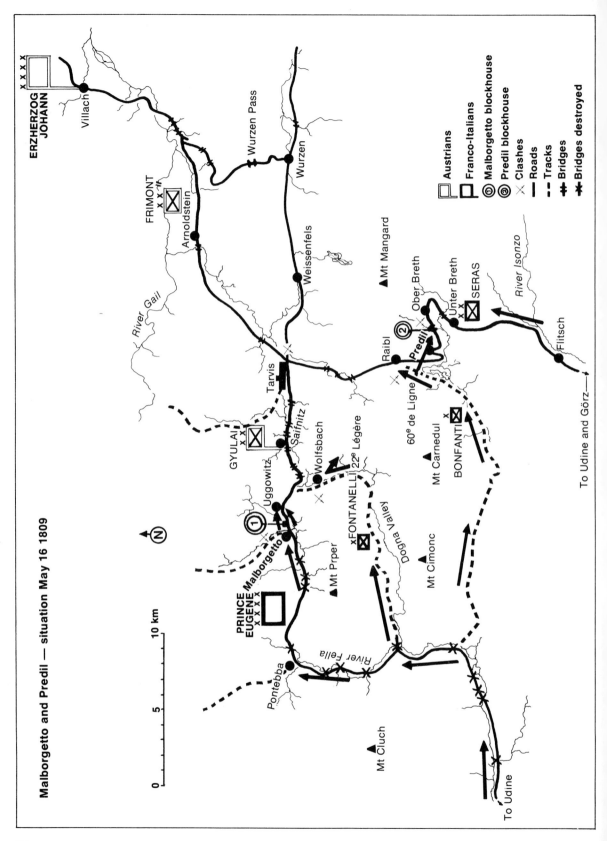

Malborgetto and Predil — situation May 16 1809

ERZHERZOG JOHANN

FRIMONT

GYULAI

PRINCE EUGENE

BONFANTI

SERAS

FONTANELLI

Villach

Arnoldstein

Wurzen Pass

Wurzen

Weissenfels

▲Mt Mangard

Ober Breth

Unter Breth

Raibl

Predil

60e de Ligne

Tarvis

Saifnitz

Wolfsbach

22e Légère

Uggowitz

▲Mt Prper

Malborgetto

Mt Carnedul

Dogna Valley

Mt Cimonc

Pontebba

River Fella

▲Mt Cluch

River Gail

River Isonzo

Flitsch

To Udine and Görz

To Udine

N

10 km

5

0

Austrians

Franco-Italians

Malborgetto blockhouse

Predil blockhouse

Clashes

Roads

Tracks

Bridges

Bridges destroyed

which ran around the perimeter wall. The Austrians countered this by manhandling one 3 pdr out of the Malborgetto Battery into the open and shelling the enemy off the hill in a very short time! That night (May 16/17) the Franco-Italians reoccupied the Buchkopf (but higher up) and built two artillery batteries — one of two cannon, the other of two cannon and a howitzer, south of Malborgetto, under the Col de Gos. They bombarded the blockhouses but were soon silenced with well-aimed fire from the 'Wiesen' and 'Zwischen' Batteries. Early on May 17 the blockhouse spur was completely surrounded by enemy infantry and at 9.30 am a general assault began in overwhelming strength.

The 'Schachtel' and 'Zwischen' Batteries fell first, then the vacant gun positions (X) and the 'Malborgetto' Battery. In a last attempt to delay the enemy advance, the Austrians set fire to Malborgetto village with artillery shells and successfully brought the advance to a halt for that day but the entire garrison was killed or captured except for three artillerymen who escaped. Franco-Italian losses were estimated at 1,000 men.

While this desperate struggle was taking place, FML Gyulai's division, which could (and should) have acted as a mobile force in support of the garrison, was being totally confused and squandered by conflicting orders from Erzherzog Johann's headquarters. Given even a modest degree of support, it is likely that the plucky garrison of the Malborgetto position could have held out for several days and have been taken off in safety at the chosen point of withdrawal.

This minor tactical cameo illustrates well the dictum 'no obstacle is effective unless it is covered by fire'. The layout of the fortified position made mutual support between the individual batteries and blockhouses difficult and there was insufficient artillery to give all-round defensive fire. By allowing the enemy to overlook the defended area and sweep it with small-arms fire, the Austrian high command sealed the fate of excellent men whom they could ill afford to lose.

If Malborgetto Blockhouse held out for 1½ days on its own, how much longer could it have been an obstacle to the Franco-Italians if Gyulai's division had been allowed to move up and support it by occupying the flanking heights and operating against the enemy?

Austrian Order of Battle

Division of FML Albert Gyulai: Infanterie-Regiment Franz Jellačić (three battalions) and Infanterie-Regiment Reisky (two battalions — one had been captured at San Daniele) under GM Gajoli; Oguliner Grenz-Infanterie-Regiment (two battalions), Szluiner Grenz-Infanterie-Regiment (one battalion) and Ott Husaren-Regiment (four squadrons) under GM Marziani; and the Marburger Landwehr (two battalions) under GM Lutz.

Mobile Corps at Villach under FML Frimont: Infanterie-Regiment St Julien, Infanterie-Regiment Strassoldo and Infanterie-Regiment Allvintzy (all of three battalions) under GM Colloredo; 1st Banal-Grenz-Infanterie-Regiment (two battalions) and four battalions of Grenadiers under GM Kleinmayrn; five battalions of Grazer Landwehr under GM Sebottendorf; plus the Husaren-Regiment Erzherzog Josef (eight squadrons) and the Husaren-Regiment Ott (four squadrons) under Oberst Boros.

Franco-Italian attacking force

Division of General de Division Durette: 22eme Légère (two battalions), 23eme Légère (four battalions), 60eme de Ligne (two battalions), 62eme de Ligne (1st and 2nd Battalions) plus six guns.

Assault on morning of May 17 at 0800 hours from Malborgetto village: against the Outwork — 1st Battalion, 62eme de Ligne (Grenadier, Voltigeur and Fusilier companies plus pioneer detachment) and 4th Battalion, 62eme de Ligne (six companies); against the Hungarian Blockhouse — 2nd Battalion, 62eme de Ligne (six companies); against the German Blockhouse — 3rd Battalion, 62eme de Ligne (six companies plus pioneer detachments, supported by artillery fire).

Assault on morning of May 17 at 0800 hours from the direction of Tarvis: two battalions of the 102eme de Ligne against the German Blockhouse and Zwischen Battery. The assault placed the Grenadier companies at the head of the column, followed by the Voltigeurs and then the Fusilier companies.

Austrian losses, according to French sources, were 75 dead and 306 captured (123 of whom were wounded); French losses, according to Austrian estimates, were 1,300 dead and wounded; French figures placed the numbers at 15 dead and 97 wounded. The truth, as usual, lies in between! □

MODELLING HMS RENOWN

Ian M. Fleming shows how to model this famous 'Force H' battleship in 1:600 scale

As an exception to the general practice in my occasional series of warship articles in *Airfix Magazine*, only one ship will be covered here: the battlecruiser *Renown,* modelled by conversion of the Airfix *Hood* kit in 1:600 scale. Readers with fingers more sensitive than mine may apply the instructions given here, *mutatis mutandis,* to the tiny 1:1200 scale of Airfix's smaller offering.

Renown was completed in September 1916, her appearance, with the usual towering layers of superstructure, then being very different from that drawn. As a battlecruiser, she had the 30-knot speed of a fast cruiser, yet was armed (though not armoured) like a 'Dreadnought' battleship. A few months earlier, at the battle of Jutland, a number of battlecruisers had been lost through being inadequately armoured, and consequently there was considerable doubt as to the wisdom of the battlecruiser concept; but *Renown*'s nine-inch armour-belt (that in contemporary 'Dreadnoughts' was 13 inches) did afford her a measure of protection. Her near-sister *Repulse,* which had joined the Grand Fleet a little earlier, had only six-inch armour, but alarm in high places was such that this was soon increased to nine inches; while *Hood,* a slightly later and larger development from *Renown*'s design, received so much additional armour that

HMS Renown *in 1944. Her appearance is as drawn, except that two twin 20 mm guns have replaced the quad pom-pom on 'B' turret. A censor has tried to obliterate the port forward HACS director and the radar aerial on the main director (IWM).*

she floated eight feet lower in the water than was originally intended!

From 1936 *Renown* underwent a three-year reconstruction at a cost of £3.5 million, only a little less than that of a new battleship of that period. Apart from her 15-inch guns, virtually nothing remained of her original upperworks; engines and funnels, bridge, gundecks, aircraft catapult and hangar, were all new when *Renown* rejoined the Home Fleet in June 1939. She also had vastly improved defence against air attack, in the form of deck armour up to 6½ inches thick, and a new battery of 20 4.5-inch AA runs as were fitted to the similarly rebuilt battleships *Queen Elizabeth* and *Valiant,* and to later Fleet Carriers.

Thus modernised, *Renown* took part in the Norwegian campaigns of 1940, before being sent to Gibraltar to serve with Force 'H'. This was, in effect, the first carrier task-force, and normally comprised a Fleet Carrier, at least one capital ship, and whatever cruisers could be spared. The initial partnership, from August 1940, was of *Ark Royal, Renown* and *Sheffield.*

After a further period with the Home Fleet *Renown* was again refitted, recommissioning in August 1943 with a huge number of 20 mm AA guns added. The aircraft and catapult had been removed to make way for a new platform to carry boats displaced by the fitting of 20 mm guns to the hangar roof, and yet more 20 mm guns. In December of that year *Renown* was sent to the Far East, now well armed against such massed aircraft attacks as had destroyed her sister *Repulse,* together with the new battleship *Prince of Wales,* two years earlier. She made her last passage in March 1945, returning to Britain from Trincomalee in a fortnight as a result of hasty recall; not required in the event, she was laid up at Portsmouth, and scrapped in 1948 after more than 30 years of illustrious service. By then she had acquired many battle-honours, including 'Atlantic' and the Cape Spartivento action in 1940, 'Mediterranean' and 'Malta Convoys' in 1941, 'Arctic' and 'North Africa' in 1942, and the bombardment of Sabang in 1944, in addition to those already mentioned.

Thus, *Renown*'s deserved fame, together with the splendid lines produced by her pre-war reconstruction, makes her a fine and useful subject for the modeller, and indeed for the wargamer. As a conversion project, she will require many alterations and additions to the *Hood* kit; but it is emphasised from the start that no part of this conversion should be beyond the reach even of the near-beginner, provided that he is prepared to follow the golden rule of all modelling — 'be patient'. This model will not be completed in a few evenings, especially if the ship is represented as in the days of her Far East servuce; the work will be much simpler, by reason of the absence of 20 mm guns and radar aerials, if the 1941 period is selected. Notes are given below for both.

Take each hull half of the *Hood* kit and saw squarely through it a little before the mid-point, and again further aft; then, discarding the central section, cement the two rear halves together, and then the forward halves to that. Ensure that the hull is of the correct length (*Renown* was 794 feet long overall = 15.88 inches in 1:600 scale), and that the sides lie flush at the join, which should be strengthened internally with thick pieces of scrap plastic. If there is any irregularity in the underwater bulges at the join, this should be dealt with using filler and — when it is completely dry — sandpaper. Next, add the armour belt, which will help to disguise and strengthen the join; this is made of 15 thou plastic card shaped to the outline shown on the drawing. As the cross-sectional drawing shows, it is faired into the hull sides at its edges. *Renown* had a more bulbous bow than *Hood*; the extension should be added from thick card cut to the outline drawn, and faired in with filler when dry. The kit has two parallel moulded lines around the hull to delimit the boot-topping appropriate to *Hood*; of these, the upper line is sanded off, and the lower used for the new waterline. Finally with regard to the hull, the scuttles and torpedo-ports are inscribed with a compass point and a steady hand.

Turning to the deck: remove the base of 'X' turret from Part 4; add Parts 5 and 6 to it, taking their position from the drawing rather than from the

Renown *in 1941* (IWM).

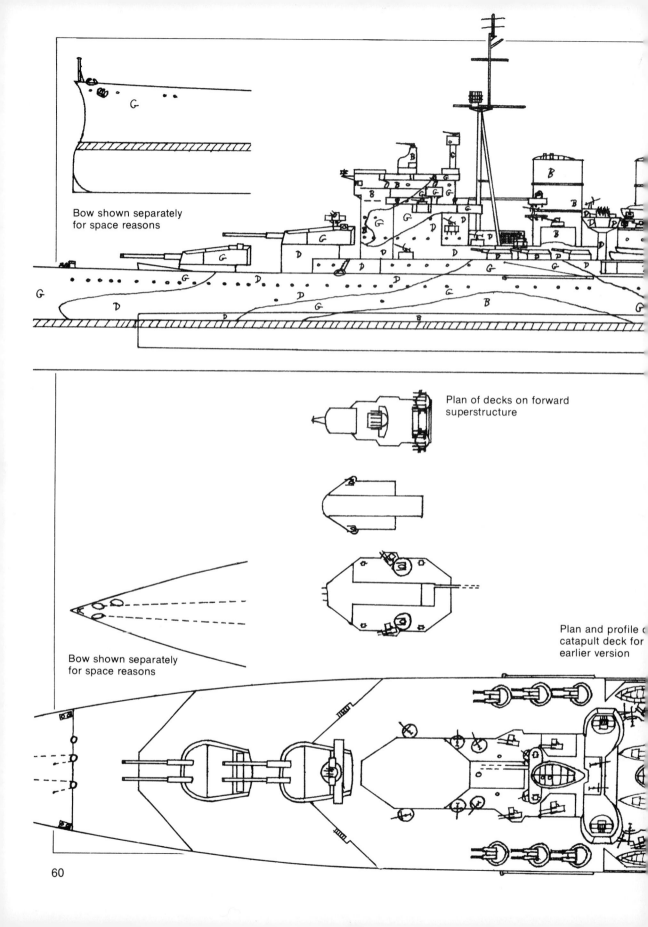

Bow shown separately
for space reasons

Plan of decks on forward
superstructure

Bow shown separately
for space reasons

Plan and profile
catapult deck for
earlier version

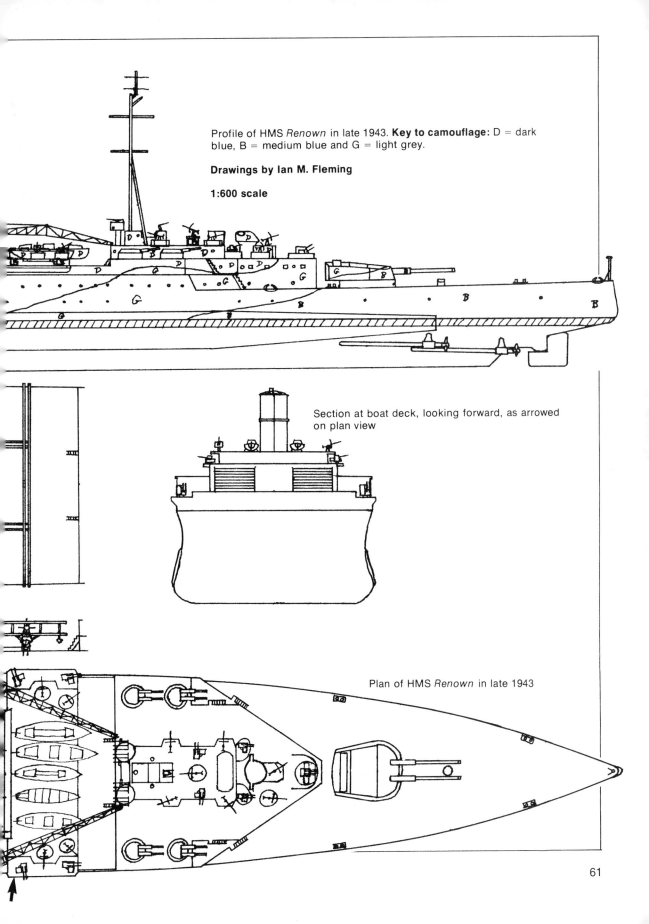

Profile of HMS *Renown* in late 1943. **Key to camouflage:** D = dark blue, B = medium blue and G = light grey.

Drawings by Ian M. Fleming

1:600 scale

Section at boat deck, looking forward, as arrowed on plan view

Plan of HMS *Renown* in late 1943

moulded locations, and cement this assembly into the hull. From Part 3, cut off and keep the foremost section before the breakwater, and also the turret bases, but discard the rest. Cement the fo'c's'le into the hull, and make up the remainder of the main deck with thick plastic card. Although only the areas before the bridge and at the catapult will be visible, it is advisable to make the whole deck right through to its junction with Parts 5 and 6, in order to provide a strong base for the superstructure. 'A' and 'B' turret bases can now be replaced on the new deck.

The aftermost area of Part 17 can easily be cut to fit into position, with new bulkheads erected on the main deck to support it. The rectangular deckhouse above it, and the mainmast base above that, are made from plastic card, as is the hangar beneath the after funnel and the crane platforms beside it.

The deck from the hangar forward to 'B' turret is next to be fitted, again supported on bulkheads from the main deck below. Do use thick card for this, as it will have to bear the bridge structure and fore-funnel. Now satisfy yourself that no flaws remain in hull or decks, and paint the whole of the model so far, while you have access to areas which will be out of reach later. From now on, it will be found best to paint each part as it is fitted.

Abreast the hangar, on the same level as the deck just fitted, is a platform extending nearly to the ship's side, on which 'nested' boats (Parts 50 and 51) appear. This platform is not supported by bulkheads, so that daylight can be seen below it before the hangar though there are low vertical screens beneath it at the main deck edge between the sides of the forward superstructure and the crane platforms.

The bridge structure, extending aft as the fore-funnel base, is built up next; detailed study of the drawing will be required for this, and careful measurement to ensure symmetry. All surfaces are flat, including the front for most of its height, but the front of the upper bridge is rounded, and contains a

row of windows. It would be quite possible to make that part from clear plastic and paint over all but the windows themselves — certainly an unusual refinement! Note also the two vision slits in each of the angled sides behind the turret, at lower bridge level.

Funnels are made from the kit parts, with strips removed from the aft edges of the halves before assembly, in order to give the streamlined appearance shown on the plan view. Very fine plastic strips are cemented around both funnels at the levels shown on the side view. A searchlight platform is fitted to the front of the fore-funnel, connected by a catwalk to the flag deck.

Kit parts also provide the 15-inch main armament; the spare turret could be used for a monitor. Note that only 'B' turret has the projecting rangefinder arms of Part 21; these should be removed from the equivalent parts on the other turrets. The eight-barrelled pom-poms (Parts 44 and 45) are mounted on a platform with thick cylindrical supports, between the funnels; a third pom-pom, made from rod and card to the same pattern, appears abaft the aft main rangefinder (Part 71). There are, unfortunately, no cranes in the *Hood* kit; if your spares box contains any, those from the *Belfast* or *Suffolk* kits will do for *Renown*; alternatively, they can be made-up from fine plastic strip, simplified if necessary. This is not as difficult as it looks!

The remainder of the armament must be made. The twin 4.5-inch guns are mounted in circular turrets, which are either carved individually or, better, moulded. This is done by pinning 20 thou plastic card to a piece of plywood in which a ¼-inch hole has been drilled, heating this and, when pliable, pushing the card through the hole with a length of dowel whose end has been suitably shaped, allow-

Force 'H', based at Gibraltar, entering the Mediterranean early in 1941. From left to right: Ark Royal, Barham and Renown. The first two were sunk by U-boats in the Med later that year (IWM).

ing for the thickness of the card. As moulding operations go, this one should present no problems.

If the ship is to be modelled as drawn, that is, as she appeared in 1943/44, you will be busy for quite a few evenings making and fitting 27 single and 18 twin 20 mm guns. (The only pair difficult to find on the drawing is that on a platform built on to the front of the fore-funnel below the searchlight platform.) Again, patience is strongly recommended here, but in my opinion the essence of modelling is that a delicate job well executed yields enormous satisfaction.

Manufacture of the various radar aerials from plastic rod is a comparatively simple matter. These are: Type 285 ('fishbone' style) on all directors; the little two-pronged Type 282 for AA barrage direction, abaft the mainmast, each side on circular platforms rising from the flag-deck, and on each side of the lower bridge; Type 281 Air Warning at the mastheads; and Type 273 Surface Warning at the top of the foremast tripod, on the 'starfish' platform (Part 86). The boat-deck abaft the hangar is the only structural item remaining; other details may be suggested by the drawing and photographs.

At that later period Renown was camouflaged in dark blue, medium blue, and light grey. Patterns may be taken from the drawing, for the port side, and the appropriate photograph for the starboard. All decks were dark grey, and topmasts and 'starfish' white.

Although this picture has been published before in Airfix Magazine, *it does show* Renown *off well in the foreground, with* Ark Royal *and* Sheffield.

If the description of *Renown* as in 1943/44 seems too daunting, the less adventurous modeller will wish to opt for the 1940/41 period when she was serving with Force 'H'. This is simply a matter of following the above instructions, but omitting — no doubt with some relief — all the 20 mm guns, and the various small platforms or extensions of platforms on which they were sited (for example, those beside the fore-funnel, and the one abaft the aft main rangefinder); all radar aerials; the quad pom-pom on 'B' turret; the tripod legs of the mainmast; and the boat platform abaft the hangar. In place of the last item, the catapult track must be fitted, together with the rails leading to it from the hangar doors; the layout is shown on a separate drawing, and the job is quickly accomplished with thick plastic strip. If there is a Walrus in your spares box, it would be a nice refinement; it is included in the *Belfast* and *Suffolk* kits. The aircraft should be camouflaged in Dark Slate Grey and Extra Dark Sea Grey, with Sky undersides, 'B' type roundels on the upper wings and 'A1' type on the hull. The ship herself was not camouflaged at this period, but plain light grey, with the main deck and the one above that scrubbed teak; and other horizontal surfaces light grey, except for the foremost area, around the anchor chains, which was dark grey. □

GERMANY'S LEOPARD

Christopher F. Foss describes this modern tank and its derivatives

The development of the Leopard 1 Main Battle Tank (MBT) can be traced back to the 1950s when the West German Army was reformed. Much of the initial equipment of the Army was supplied from the United States, including large numbers of M47 medium tanks. The Germans soon started a project to develop their own tank, but in fact before the German Army issued a requirement for a new MBT, Daimler-Benz had already designed one to meet the requirements of the Indian Army. However, this design was not successful and the Indian Army awarded the contract to the British company of Vickers, who developed the Vickers 37-ton MBT which is now being built in India, and has also been adopted by Kenya and Kuwait.

Two German Groups, designated Group A and Group B, were awarded development contracts.

The first Group A prototype was completed in June 1960, while the first Group B prototype was completed in May 1960. At an early stage it was decided to concentrate on the Group A vehicles. This Group, which comprised Atlas MaK, Jung, Luther, Jordan and Porsche, built a total of 30 prototype vehicles, followed by a pre-production batch of 50 tanks. These were tested both in Germany and abroad, and most of the problems normally associated with the introduction of a new vehicle into service were found and corrected long before the first production tank was completed.

In 1963, Krauss-Maffei of Munich were appointed General-Contractor for the management and series production of the Leopard MBT. Krauss-Maffei has been associated with the design, development and production of armoured fighting vehicles for over 40 years. In 1934 the company was nominated prime contractor for the SdKfz 7 8-ton half-track,

Leopard A2 MBT.

and was also involved on the VK601 light reconnaissance tank and the VK1801 infantry support tank; neither of the latter vehicles were built in very large numbers.

Production

The first production Leopard 1 MBT was completed on September 9 1965, and since then over 6,000 tanks of all variants have been ordered. While Krauss-Maffei build the basic MBT, and more recently the Gepard anti-aircraft tank, production of the Leopard armoured recovery vehicle, armoured engineer vehicle and the Biber bridge-layer, has been undertaken by MaK of Kiel.

Current contracts will keep the Munich production line busy until at least 1980 and there is every possibility that other countries will place additional orders which will keep the production line open until the early 1980s.

Krauss-Maffei is now tooling up for the production of the Leopard 2 MBT, and the first of 1,800 will be completed in 1979. Krauss-Maffei will build 990 tanks, while Atlas MaK will build the remaining 810 tanks. The Leopard 2 will replace the large number of old American M48 tanks which have now been in service with the German Army for 20 years.

The MBT family

The German Army has a total of 2,437 Leopard MBT's in service. These are:

Leopard A1 (1,845) These have recently been modernised and now have a thermal sleeve for main armament, stabilisation system which allows the main armament to be fired on the move, new tracks, rubber side skirts, modified turret hatches, modified deep-wading equipment and additional armour added to the sides and rear of the turret. These now have the designation Leopard A1A1.

Leopard A2 (232) These were built with a turret of stronger cast steel, a more efficient exhaust filtration system, improved NBC protection and passive-image intensification equipment for the commander and driver.

Leopard A3 (110) This has the new turret of spaced armour which incorporates a wedge-shaped welded mantlet, turret stowage included in the contour of the turret, and the loader's periscope which is adjustable in both elevation and azimuth. This model also incorporates the modifications of the A2 model.

Leopard A4 (250) This was the final batch of Leopard 1 MBTs built for the German Army and is similar to the A3 but has an integrated fire control system and a fully automatic gearbox.

Export models

Australia These MBTs have the Belgian SABCA fire control system which incorporates a laser rangefinder, external stowage boxes and a tropical kit. Some have also been fitted with a dozer blade.

Top Close-up of smoke dischargers and additional armour on Leopard A1A1. **Above** Close-up of Leopard A1A1 showing anti-aircraft machine-gun mounting and additional armour. **Below** Rear of Leopard MBT.

for military modellers

Top *Leopard A3.* **Above** *Leopard A2 on right alongside an A3.* **Below** *Leopard A4.*

Belgium First deliveries were made to Belgium in February 1968. These are also being refitted with the SABCA fire control system and have the Belgian FN machine-gun rather than the German MG3.

Canada These have the SABCA fire control system and an American passive periscope for the gunner and driver.

Denmark These have external stowage boxes on the sides of the hull and the three driver's periscopes each have a wiper blade and a washer.

Italy Krauss-Maffei supplied Italy with 200 Leopard tanks, the first of these being delivered in April 1971. The Italian company of Oto Melara has since built a further 600 vehicles under licence.

Netherlands The first Dutch Leopard MBT was delivered in July 1969. These have external stowage boxes on the hull sides and different smoke dischargers.

Norway The first Norwegian Leopard MBT was delivered in January 1969.

Leopard variants

Armoured recovery vehicle It was decided at an early stage that an armoured recovery vehicle was required to operate with the Leopard 1 MBTs and that this would use the same chassis. The first production Leopard ARV, or Bergepanzer Standard, was completed by MaK of Kiel in September 1966. This has a new superstructure forward of the engine compartment which protects the crew from small arms fire. Mounted at the front of the hull is the dozer blade, which is used for clearing obstacles on the battlefield, and for stabilising the vehicle when the crane is being used. The latter is mounted on the right side of the hull and can be traversed through 270 degrees. Maximum lifting capacity is 20,000 kg. This crane is used to change tank guns, turrets and engines. A Leopard ARV normally carries a replacement Leopard engine on the rear of the superstructure. The record for a complete engine change on a Leopard MBT is just under ten minutes. The ARV also has a winch for recovery operations which has a capacity of 35,000 kg. Armament consists of a 7.62 mm MG3 anti-aircraft machine-gun and a similar weapon is mounted in the bow. Smoke dischargers are also provided. More recently an improved model of the vehicle has been developed (called the Leopard ARV Product Improved), which has been designed for use with the heavier Gepard anti-aircraft tank and the new Leopard 2, both of which are heavier than the normal Leopard 1 MBT. The major external difference is a large jack mounted at the rear of the hull on the right side.

Armoured engineer vehicle This is identical to the ARV but has the following modifications. In place of the spare engine an auger is carried on the rear engine decking. This is used to bore holes in the ground and the dozer blade can also be fitted with special teeth to rip up roads. Explosives are carried for demolition purposes and a heat exchanger is installed.

Top *Close-up of A4 turret.* **Above** *Dutch CA1 anti-aircraft tank.*

Bridgelayer Biber After trials with two different prototypes in 1969, again designated model A and model B, one model was selected for production. Production of this commenced in 1973 for the German Army. When extended the bridge is 22 metres long. An advantage of the Biber over the British Chieftain, French AMX-30 and American M48/M60 bridgelayers, is that the bridge opens out horizontally rather than vertically which reduces the chance of detection by the enemy while the bridge is being positioned.

for military modellers

Above *A Belgian Leopard on manoeuvres.* **Left** *Bergepanzer Leopard* (Bundesministerium der Verteidigung). **Below left** *Leopard 155 mm self-propelled gun.*

Leopard 155 mm self-propelled gun This was developed as a private venture in 1973 by Krauss-Maffei and the GIAT and is basically a Leopard 1 MBT chassis with its turret replaced by the complete turret of the 155 mm GCT self-propelled gun. The turret can be traversed through a full 360 degrees, and elevated from −5 degrees to +66 degrees. A total of 42 rounds of ammunition are carried, and these can be fired at the rate of eight rounds per minute. For anti-aircraft defence, a 7.62 mm machine-gun is mounted on top of the turret.

Leopard training tank This is a Leopard hull with an instructor's cabin in place of the turret. The turret has all round vision and accommodates the instructor and two additional student drivers who can hear the instructor's direction to the driver over the intercom. The instructor can take over control of the vehicle at any time. This version has the same weight and can ford to the same depth as the MBT.

Gepard anti-aircraft tank The Gepard has been developed as the replacement for the old M42 self-propelled anti-aircraft guns which have now been in service with the German Army for 20 years. It is based on a modified Leopard 1 chassis, this being slightly longer (80 mm) and having thinner armour than the MBT.

Main armament comprises twin 35 mm fully automatic cannon mounted in a turret with a traverse of 360 degrees, the guns having an elevation of +85 degrees and a depression of −5 degrees. A total of 640 rounds of anti-aircraft ammunition are carried plus a further 40 rounds of armour-piercing ammunition for use against armoured vehicles. Four smoke dischargers are mounted on either side of the turret.

The fire control system includes a search radar mounted on the rear of the turret and a tracking radar mounted on the front of the turret. When not in action the search radar folds down behind the back of the turret while the tracking radar can be

Top *Biber bridgelayer with bridge extended.* **Above** *Gepard anti-aircraft tank.*

traversed through 180 degrees so that it faces the turret. The Dutch vehicles (designated CA1) have a Dutch-designed fire control system. There can be little doubt that the Gepard is the best self-propelled anti-aircraft gun in the world, but is rather expensive at just under £2 million per vehicle.

Other variants

Currently undergoing trials is a new bridgelayer which is similar to the Biber except that once the bridge is in the horizontal position, legs unfold at the far end of the bridge into the vertical position. At the end of each leg is a circular base plate which stops the leg sinking into the river or ditch bed. When the first bridge has been laid the vehicle withdraws to the rear and the procedure is repeated until the obstacle is crossed.

Another variant undergoing trials is the Pionier-panzer 2(GPM), prototypes of which have been completed by MaK and EWK. This vehicle has been designed for preparing river crossings and has had its turret replaced by one or two hydraulically operated shovels on long arms.

There have also been numerous projected versions of the Leopard which have not even been built and these include a Roland SAM vehicle and another along the lines of the World War 2 Jagd-panther tank destroyer. Mention must also be made of the Leopard chassis which is being used as a trials unit for the German RS-80 multiple rocket system. □

for military modellers

Simple 54mm figure conversions

Robert C. Gibson illustrates some basic modifications to Airfix figure kits

Some years ago, when I was just starting in model soldiers, the price of a metal figure was beyond my means. At that time, I used to buy whatever plastic figures I could find and convert them to the ones I wanted. The important thing about these early efforts is that they showed me that with skill and patience, the humblest toy figure could become a collector's standard figure.

While I still use plastic figures made by Britains and some other manufacturers, the principal source is Airfix 1:32 scale products and it is these that this article is all about. The quality of the figures does vary depending on the age of the offering — for example, most of the 'standard' World War 2 sets are the oldest (but not all of them) and the Waterloo sets are much newer.

The preparation of these figures can be separated into three stages: Improving the basic figure; altering the basic figure and building on the basic figure. However, before embarking on any cutting or carving, take the figure or figures you have chosen through your reference library and make a note of what work you need to do.

Improving the basic figure

Most of the figures need a certain amount of trimming and the moulding flash removing. Start at the feet and cut the flash away evenly in one long line. If this proves difficult because of creases in the clothing or equipment, cut upwards to a point where a cut at right angles is possible, eg edges of clothing, straps. A little care is needed where the flash line runs next to fine engraving; for example parallel to the engraving on the Guardsman's bearskin or across epaulette straps.

Once the moulding flash is removed, some attention can be paid to other areas. Due to the moulding process, arms, muskets and the like are often unnaturally joined to the body of the figure. The best way to tackle these is to work inwards cutting away a little at a time. With items such as sword and bayonet scabbards, cut away under the scabbard to the correct thickness first, and then carefully cut away the superfluous plastic underneath, little by little. You may find the need to improve parts of the moulding, eg epaulette fringes where the detail

sometimes disappears towards the centre. Again, neat clean cuts are the order of the day.

For the purists, the French Guard Grenadiers are in a mixture of dress, and the *cartouche* (cartridge pouch) at the rear is too small. As the rest of the figure is basically in full dress as it was interpreted for battle, the pouch could reasonably be covered with a white cover. Therefore, the engraved eagle can be removed and the pouch covered with a strip of writing paper cut to the same width and shape as the flap but 3 mm longer. A roll of Plasticine will simulate the rolled fatigue cap carried under the pouch. Alternatively, a plume can be added to the bearskin to bring the figure up to parade dress, and the existing cartridge pouch retained or replaced by a Historex spare.

Something else to look for at this stage is what I call 'disappearing detail'. This happens particularly with belts and straps. Check under the arms and at the backs of the figures to ensure that the straps follow where they should. Use your reference sources to help you here and make sure that items like the shoulder straps of knapsacks reappear where they should. Either cut into the uniform to make them reappear, or make new straps out of notepaper. Where new straps have to be fitted, start them at a suitable 'junction', eg where they appear from under the epaulette or shoulder ornaments of the uniform, or at a crossing point.

The British Line Infantry officer in the Waterloo set has no shoulder belt at the back. As the figure is too slender to cut into, a new strap has to be fitted between the right shoulder and the sash at the right hip. A very slight curve is needed in the belt if it is to fit well, but with the vigorous pose a certain amount of separation from the body across the back is permissible.

Note This figure can only be used as it comes for a Light Company officer, since the curved light-cavalry style sabre was not usually carried by Grenadier Company officers, who favoured the straight sword called *degen* by the Germans and *epée* by the French. However if you can find a genuine example of a sabre-bearing Grenadier officer, feel free!

Once you have completed the initial stage of pre-

Left to right *Drummer, Grenadiers of the French Imperial Guard, rear view; Grenadier of the French Imperial Guard with beer mug; Sergeant, Chasseurs of the French Imperial Guard, rear view.*

Left to right *Drummer, Grenadiers of the French Imperial Guard, front view; Grenadier of the French Imperial Guard, ten years' service; Sergeant, Light Infantry Carabiniers in 1812-style coatee and bearskin.*

paration, you may wish to start painting. If your fancy lies in altering the figure further, read on.

Altering the basic figure

Quite a few of the Airfix 1:32 scale figures can be simply altered to cover soldiers of other companies, regiments, countries.

French Guard Grenadier to Dutch Guard Grenadier This conversion is perhaps the simplest. All that is required is the covering of the brass plate on the front of the bearskin. The easiest way is to build over it with Plasticine, carefully grooving it to match the fur above and around it with a sharp blade. Treat the Plasticine with banana oil (obtainable from your local model shop) using a paint brush and brushing vertically so as to retain the fur texture. Once the banana oil is dry, you can proceed to the painting stage.

French Guard Grenadier to French Guard Chasseur This involves modifying the bearskin and some trimming with the knife. The bearskin plate must be covered as before and this time the patch at the top of the bearskin as well. Leave the small tassel uncovered. With a sharp knife, remove the grenade ornaments from the turnbacks and trim the lapels so that the edges are no longer curved but vertical, falling straight down to the top edge of the turnback. After treatment, the figure is ready to prepare for painting. Both the above figures have somewhat undersized blanket rolls. These can be built up with Plasticine: the straps can be cut from writing paper, but note that grooves should be cut for them to fit into as the straps would be tightened to retain the roll. Add the coiled part afterwards, again cut from writing paper. These represent the excess left after the straps were tightened.

One figure that will need treatment before it can be painted is the French Guard Grenadier drummer. For reasons best known to the manufacturers, this figure has been produced with both epaulettes and the padded wings peculiar to musicians of continental armies, and two sets of lapels. Whatever the reason, it works to our advantage since the lapels and shoulder decorations can be cut away or reworked to suit different regiments.

Guard Grenadier Drummer To produce the 'standard' figure, some cutting is necessary. First the padded wings under the epaulettes are removed, then the outer lapels removed. The plume can be removed for full dress, or replaced for parade dress. Quite effective plumes can be made from pipe cleaners treated with polystyrene cement; the advantage of this method is that by stripping the bottom 2 mm to 3 mm of the plume down to the bare wire, and twisting the wire so that it can be plugged into the headgear, a strong joint is assured.

Guard Chasseur Drummer Again, the padded wings are removed and this time also the inner lapels. The bearskin is treated as for the French Guard Chasseur, and the grenade ornaments on the turnbacks removed. The plume is either removed or replaced as for the Guard Grenadier drummer.

Grenadier Drummer, 42nd Line Regiment 1808-10 This figure is similar to the Guard Grenadier. From top to bottom: the bearskin is the same as the Dutch Grenadier. The shoulder pads are cut away, as are the outer lapels, but this time the tassels on the buttonholes are removed, and the grenade on the drum belt also. A longer apron is required, suspended from a belt just below the waistcoat — this can be cut from writing paper and fixed over the existing apron.

Colour details are as follows: Bearskin — black fur, red patch with white grenade, cords and tassels white, red plume; Coatee — sky blue with yellow collar, cuffs and lapels, laced in yellow. White turnbacks, sky blue cuff patches, both laced yellow; Epaulettes — red; Breeches — white;

Bearskins

A   B   C   D   E

Bearskins of the French Imperial Army 1804-1815. **A and B** The most common style, used by the Guard Grenadiers, but also by the Grenadiers and Vélite-Grenadiers of the Italian Royal Guard, and some Line Infantry grenadiers with differing front plates. **C and D** Rear and front of the second most common style — used by the Chasseurs of the Imperial Guard and Carabiniers of Light Infantry. Style D with a patch similar to Style A (hence Style D/A) with Style D/C was commonly used by Elite Companies of Line Dragoons. **E** Style E/A was used by the Elite Gendarmerie (foot and mounted) of the Imperial Guard, and the Foot Artillery of the Guard.

Cartridge pouch — Notepaper cover

Covered pickelhaube — Build around pin with plastic putty; Cut away around ear

Blanket roll — Cut — Build up with Plasticine

British knapsack conversion — Trim with sharp knife — Build over top with Plasticine — Etch hide grain with knife point

US Marine conversion Blend the new lower trouser with existing curves — Build up over the gaiters with Plasticine — Allow trouser bottoms to flop over boots

British stovepipe shako — Pipe cleaner 'plume' — Flat top — Build up top with Plasticine — Carefully remove side plume

Drawings by author

Gloves — white; Gaiters — white (Parade Dress — with plume), black (Full Dress — without plume).

Whilst the Guard Grenadiers do provide ample scope for conversions, there are others.

British Line Grenadier 1809-12 To produce this figure, careful alteration of the shako is needed. First, the plume is carefully removed, leaving the cords intact. Second a new plume must be made and fixed to the front of the shako at the top — pipecleaner plumes are especially useful here. Third, the shako is built up to the level of the front with a flat top, using Plasticine which is then 'fixed' with polystyrene cement or banana oil, so the figure is ready for painting.

German Dragoon in Manoeuvre Order 1895 For this figure, the advancing German (World War 2) Infantry figure is used. After trimming, all the pockets are cut off, together with all straps and pouches — leave the waist belt, but clean of pouches. You should now have a figure with a simple tunic. Now remove the magazine from the rifle, and cut the helmet away around the ears, so that the front and rear visors are separate. The front visor should curve upwards over the ear; the rear visor is cut square. The spike is added using a pin embedded centrally in the top of the helmet, and built up using plastic putty. As we are aiming at a covered *pickelhaube,* the spike should be conical. Add the shoulder straps (cut from very thin plastic card) then the pouch belt (again from plastic card) over the left shoulder and down to the right hip, leaving space for the small pouch. Once the belt is secure, pin the pouch in position.

Colour details are as follows: Helmet — light khaki with a red band 3 mm wide round the middle. Black leather chinstrap; Tunic — sky-blue. Yellow straight cuffs and collar. Yellow piping down front of tunic and on pockets at rear. Shoulder straps yellow with red crown over a Gothic monogram 'A'. Buttons brass; Breeches — very dark grey; Boots — black leather; Belts — white; Pouch — black leather with oval brass plate; Carbine — dark brown wood, brass butt plate and blackened steel barrel and mechanism.

US Marine Corps Raider 1943 Remove all equipment except the waist belt, water bottle and magazine pouch from the sub-machine gunner. Build up the trousers over the gaiters, working in the creases with the handle of a paint brush to give a loose baggy effect, using Plasticine.

Colour details are as follows: Jacket, trousers and helmet cover — pale khaki drill with faded olive green and dark brown patches overall; Belt and pouches — pale khaki; Helmet strap — dark brown leather; Sub-machine gun — blackened steel; Water bottle top — blackened tin; Boots — brown, weathered and dusty.

Building on the basic figure

This stage is all about adding and subtracting — changing heads, bodies and equipment about to make a completely different figure, or a change of pose. The most obvious of these changes that spring to mind is a head swop. Using the Guard Grenadier set and a shako-topped head, the regiments of the Middle Guard and most of the French Line Regiments from 1807 to 1812 become possible with some added work. This head change can be done in two ways — first by using a head taken from another Airfix figure, or second by introducing a 'spare' head. The latter method is very useful if you can't get a head with suitable headgear by swopping — both Historex and Rose do bare heads in various styles, and Rose do a bandaged head. But let's start with a simple one.

Guard Grenadier raising beer mug For this we need a Phoenix spare — a beer mug — and the Guard Grenadier figure at ease pointing with his right hand. After trimming the figure, remove the pointing finger. Then, measuring the handle against the hand, cut away the middle part but not enough to fit over the hand. Bend the broken ends slightly outwards; bore two holes in the top and bottom of the hand, and clamp the handle over the hand gently with a pair of pliers. Using tube polystyrene cement, fill the top of the beer mug and trickle the overflow over the hand to seal the joint. After that, carry on painting — Vive l'Empereur!

Head swopping is a delicate operation: use a very thin razor blade to ensure a clean and level cut. For Airfix heads, use a pin cut down to secure the new head, and fill the gap with polystyrene cement.

Light Infantry Carabinier, 1812 Some Light Infantry regiments of the French Army retained their bearskins after the introduction of the 1811 regulations, which specified the shako — our figure depicts a sergeant of one of these regiments. The body of a French Line Infantryman is used, together with the head of a Guard Grenadier. After the head is fitted, it is treated as for a Guard Chasseur. The decorations are removed from the cartridge pouch and coat skirts. The blanket roll above the knapsack is enlarged with Plasticine and straps are added from writing paper. Depending on the figure, an extra crossbelt may need to be added, again from writing paper. Whatever the figure, a sword and bayonet cluster will have to be added — in this case I borrowed one from a Guard Grenadier and pinned it in place, using a small pinhead to simulate the stud which secured the sword scabbard to the belt frog.

(Colour note: The uniform is standard except the epaulettes which are silver and red mixed with red straps (and are, of course, built up from Plasticine) and the chevrons above the cuffs and the bearskin tassel are silver).

If you are fitting a Historex or Rose head, you will need to bore a hole to fit the head into. Do this carefully so that you obtain a tight fit, especially for polystyrene heads as a too liberal use of cement can cause disaster. Both cases will need a smear of polystyrene cement to secure them in position.

Bavarian Infantryman, 1848 This is an unusual subject, with a 'modern' uniform and Napoleonic accoutrements. The basic figure needed is a kneeling or standing British Line Infantryman 1815, and a Rose Bavarian head of the 1870 period. The figure is first decapitated and the shoulder wings (but not the shoulder straps) are carefully removed. Remove all cuff detail and any braid on the front of the coatee. Trim away the gaiters below the trouser bottoms. Next, cut the neck so that the head can be fitted, and fit the head, liberally coating the plug part with polystyrene cement. Once the head is firmly secured, and not before, build up the coatee skirts at the front and sides to the same level as at the back with Plasticine. Trim the knapsack straps leaving two 5 mm long straps in the centre, then build up the top over the blanket roll to give a bigger 'lid' with Plasticine, but leaving the straps

Top left *Bavarian infantryman, 2nd Regiment, 1848.* **Top right** *Schwarzburg infantryman, 1845.* **Above left** *Prussian dismounted dragoon wearing helmet cover and band (Manöverkappe), 8th Regiment, 1895.* **Above right** *Bavarian infantryman, 7th Regiment, 1870. Note that both above figures have been produced from the same original, ie, the advancing German (World War 2) infantryman.*

visible. Fix both areas with banana oil or polystyrene cement, and you are ready to paint.

Colour details are as follows: Helmet — black leather, brass chinstrap and oval front plate with the Bavarian lion on it. Black fur crest. White/blue/white circular cockade above left ear; Coatee/Tunic — sky-blue, piped red down the front. (2nd Infantry Regiment) Black collar and cuffs, piped red. Red shoulder straps with yellow number '2'. Brass buttons; Cross belts — white; Haversack and belt — buff; Pouch — black leather, with a crowned brass plate pierced with a monogram 'L'; Boots — black leather; Musket — dark brown wood, steel barrel and lock, brass fittings; Knapsack-dark brown hide.

Painting your figure

I have experimented with a number of undercoats over the years, and found the best method is to use an aerosol, usually the type sold for use on cars (it's much cheaper). White is the best, since it highlights any deficiencies in the construction work before it is too late. When spraying, use the spray sparingly to avoid dripping paint, but cover thoroughly. The choice of the colour paint is a personal choice: I leave it up to you. □

HUNGARIAN ARTILLERY 1939-1945

Terry Gander sheds light on a neglected but important aspect of the war

For an article on Hungarian artillery to appear in an English modelling publication may seem to many to be an odd, or even esoteric event, but the truth is that it should not be. For too many years now military enthusiasts have been sated with a mass of material on the campaigns in North Africa, the Pacific and North-West Europe, and only now is the average reader beginning to realise that the most important and far-reaching campaigns and battles took place on the Eastern Front, and in the USSR. Of late more and more books and articles have become available in the West regarding those campaigns and the continuing dominance of the Soviet Union in Eastern Europe some 30 years after the war ended can only serve to reinforce the importance of the war in the East. While I can only leave the reader to discover the various facets and aspects of that massive conflict, I have decided to delve into one small area of that war and the part

---

Title photo 47 mm 36 M, here seen in its original Belgian form and manned by Belgians. The Hungarian version was identical. Below 40 mm 40 M.

taken by one arm of one country, namely the artillery used by the Hungarian Army.

Hungary, populated for many centuries by the fiercely independent Magyars, has had a very stormy history and for a long time has had to fight for what little autonomy it could muster. The Depression hit Hungary just as hard as it did the rest of Europe during the early 1930s and as a result the Hungarian state fell increasingly under the commercial influence of Nazi Germany to whom the abundant Hungarian corn harvests were exported in exchange for manufactured goods. By 1941 Hungary was virtually a vassal state of Germany, but in name only for, despite the dictatorship which prevailed in Hungary, it remained a fairly liberal one and small opposition parties were tolerated. During 1941 the Hungarian armies were included in the plans for Operation Barbarossa and they formed part of the army formations that formed the southern part of the front.

At first the Hungarian contingent consisted of one Army Group with a large percentage of cavalry. The army was well-equipped, on paper at least, but very often there were no equipment reserves or repair facilities. Over the years the Hungarian Army had tried to become self-sufficient and manufactured many items such as rifles and sub-machine-guns, and even machine-guns for the few tanks they put in the field in 1941. But with artillery the Hungarians were not so advanced. One of the main reasons for this was the usual abundance of useful artillery pieces left over from the Great War. The break-up of the old Austro-Hungarian Empire ensured that Hungary got a fair share of the residue that remained in the gun parks and many of these old pieces were still in service in 1941. But by using the old facilities set up by Skoda before 1918 the Hungarians were able to undertake a modest programme of updating and modernising the old equipment and by 1940 they were actually in a position to undertake the design, development and licence manufacture of modern artillery.

Above *75 mm 15 M. In this form the Skoda M 15 was one of the most widely-used mountain guns ever produced.* **Right** *75 mm 15/35 M (picture courtesy F. Kosar).* **Below right** *80 mm 5/8 M.* **Bottom** *10.5 cm 37 M.*

A survey of the artillery equipment in use in Hungary between 1941 and 1944 provides a most interesting and unusual array of designs of all ages. Starting with the smallest artillery calibres, the first gun to be considered is the German 3.7 cm Pak 35/36 known to the Hungarians as the 37 mm 36 M. Numbers of these were sold to Hungary in 1936 in exchange for wheat and in 1941 they formed the backbone of the Hungarian anti-tank defences. They were usually issued to infantry formations and there they doubled as infantry guns firing small HE shells at strongpoints and similar targets. By 1940 the Army expansion meant that more anti-tank guns were needed but by then Germany was in no position to supply more. The Hungarians decided to make their own, but their end result was an unusual one. Some 36 M carriages had their worn barrels replaced by 40 mm barrels produced on the

for military modellers

Above 10.5 cm 40 M. **Below** 10.5 cm 31 M. Used in small numbers only, the 10.5 cm 31 M was deployed as a long-range heavy gun. **Bottom** 15 cm 31 M.

machine tools set up to turn out Bofors 40 mm anti-aircraft barrels (of which more later). In this manner the 40 mm 40 M was produced and issued in small numbers. Another anti-tank gun import was the Belgian Canon de 47 SA-FRC which became the 47 mm 36 M but only small numbers were involved. But whereas the Belgians used small tracked vehicles to tow these guns the Hungarians used horses as the guns were intended for use by cavalry units. Thus a limber had to be used and the 47 mm 36 M became an awkward and heavy load, so by 1941 it was used by reserve and second-line units only.

Once Hungary was in the thick of the fighting on its sectors of the Russian Front, its forces began to lose equipment in large amounts. On many occasions the Hungarians took some fearful maulings and during 1942 they were often singled out by the Soviets to take the spearpoint of any new attacks. To keep their allies in the line the Germans had to divert some of their own weapons to the Hungarians and among these were numbers of the 5 cm Pak 38 and 7.5 cm Pak 40. Of the two the 5 cm guns were the most important numerically and became the 50 mm 38 M. The 7.5 cm guns were issued in smaller numbers and became the 75 mm 40 M.

Among the artillery left to the new Hungarian Army after 1920 were numbers of the Skoda M15 mountain gun. These handy little guns became the 75 mm 15 M but they were designed as pack guns and were thus of only limited use to the Hungarians. In about 1930 they needed a light cavalry gun and the 15 M carriage was altered to suit the new role. The barrel and cradle were unchanged but the rest of the carriage was modified to suit it for horse traction. By the time the changes had been made a new designation was needed and the 75 mm 15/31 M was issued. But it was considerably heavier than the original and six horses were needed to tow a relatively small gun. So more changes were made to produce the 75 mm 15/35 M, but these were mainly issued to mountain artillery units where they were towed by only four horses.

The bulk of the Hungarian field artillery was issued with the old Skoda M 5/8 field gun. This was an 80 mm gun that had been in production at the old Skoda plant in Hungary during the Great War and in 1941 it was still in use as the 8 cm 5/8 M. It was an entirely conventional design. To back up these guns there came a variety of pieces with larger calibres. One of the oldest was the 10 cm 14a M, the old Skoda 100 mm M14. Some minor changes had been made to these howitzers to suit Hungarian requirements but by 1941 few were left as they had been replaced by an imported howitzer, namely the German 10.5 cm leFH 18. Numbers of these had been bought from Germany in 1937 and they became the 10.5 cm 37 M. Made by Rheinmetall-Borsig, these guns were virtually identical to the German service model but differed in some respects, the most noticeable of which were the wheels.

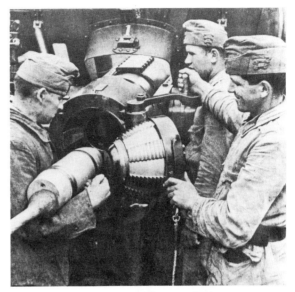

Gunners training on a 15 cm 31 M. These shots will be very useful for anyone wishing to make a model of this howitzer using Ken Musgrave's drawing. The uniform overalls appear to be a light khaki with brown leather belts.

The use of the German 10.5 cm as a 'standard' artillery calibre prompted the Hungarians to opt for the same calibre themselves and during the late 1930s they began to design and develop their own howitzer. The end result was the 10.5 cm 40 M, produced at the MAVAG works. The MAVAG concern was the Hungarian State Railway and their plant was chosen for the task as not only did they have the space and buildings suitable for weapon production but they had, in the past, been concerned with many of the artillery modernisation programmes completed to date. Although entirely conventional and unadventurous, the 40 M was not produced in other than very small numbers. After a few complete equipments had been made and issued the assembly line was diverted to producing a special version of the 40 M for fitting into the Hungarian 'Zrynyl' assault gun, and in all 72 guns were made.

for military modellers

21 cm 40 M. The most noticeable modifications to the original 39 M are the larger wheels and the strengthening rod across the trail legs.

To back up the 105 mm howitzers were small numbers of another import, the Bofors 105 mm Model 1931 gun. To the Hungarians it was the 10.5 cm 31 M and the counterpart to another Bofors import, the 15 cm 31 M — both used the same carriage. These two pieces formed the modern backbone of the Hungarian Army in Russia and despite their lack of uniformity with other German and allied equipment, they were used widely on the Eastern Front. Both pieces were solid and reliable designs with few frills and, unlike some of the other Hungarian 'updated' guns, they proved eminently suitable for mechanised warfare.

Chief of the Hungarian 'updates' was the Skoda 149 mm M 14. Numbers of these were among the residue of the old Empire armies which became part of the early Hungarian gun park, and in 1941 small numbers were still in use as the 15 cm 14 M. In 1935 these howitzers were altered to improve range and handling. The old barrels were renovated and to accommodate new ammunition a muzzle brake was fitted, the result becoming the 15 cm 14/35 M. Later still more changes were made both to the 14 M and the 14/35 M to produce the 14/39 M which had an improved muzzle brake, some carriage changes and other minor alterations, especially to the cradle. Although used in smaller numbers than the more modern Bofors pieces, the revamped Skoda howitzers gave good service and at times were even used by German artillery units fighting alongside the Hungarians.

One result of a commercial alliance with Italy was that at one stage between the wars, Hungary was considered to be an Italian 'sphere of influence' but on the military side there was little to show for this in 1941, by which time the two nations had little contact with each other. One military transaction which did take place, however, was the sale of the STAM/Ansaldo Obice da 210/22 modello 35. Exactly why this howitzer was sold to Hungary at a time when the Italian forces were crying out for modern equipment is now not clear but the first equipments were delivered in 1939. The Hungarian designation for these original equipments was 21 cm 39 M, but once in service they proved to be less than satisfactory as their carriages proved to be too weak for prolonged use and towing. The Hungarians made their own alterations to the carriage and changed the designation to 21 cm 40 M, but not long after that they began to produce their own equipments as the 21 cm 40a M — not many, perhaps about 12, appear to have been made.

At the top end of the calibre scale in the Hun-

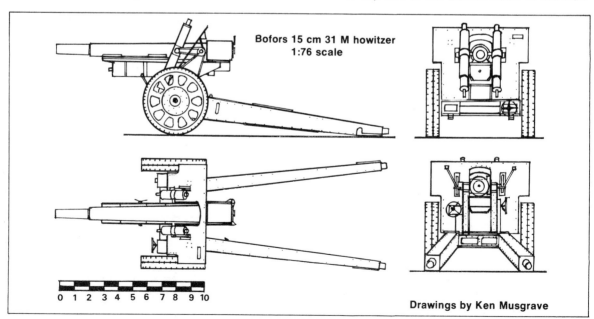

Bofors 15 cm 31 M howitzer
1:76 scale

0 1 2 3 4 5 6 7 8 9 10

Drawings by Ken Musgrave

Above *15 cm 14/39 M.* **Right, below and bottom right** *30.5 cm 16 M ready for the road. The three loads consist of the barrel, the cradle and the main carriage bed.*

garian gun park was a Great War veteran, the 30.5 cm 16 M, originally the Skoda M 11/16 howitzer. Exactly how many of these monsters were used by the Hungarians is now uncertain but it was probably not more than four, and it seems unlikely that they saw much service.

On the anti-aircraft front, the Hungarian range of equipment was relatively restricted. At the lower end of the calibre range was the Danish Madsen 2 cm Model 1933, otherwise the 20 mm 33 M. Another Scandinavian country, Sweden, supplied the rest of the Hungarian anti-aircraft artillery. In 1929 a number of 8 cm Model 1929 anti-aircraft guns were delivered to Hungary and in 1941 these formed the main anti-aircraft defences of Hungary itself, as the 8 cm 29 M (in 1939 another modernisation programme changed this designation to 8 cm 29/38 M but the alterations were minor). As a design the 29 M was unremarkable, but it has a small place in history as one of the early results of the Bofors/Krupp association which eventually led to the famous German 8.8 cm Flak series.

Hungary was one of the first nations to take out a licence to manufacture the Bofors 40 mm anti-aircraft gun, and as a result of licences taken out in 1935 and 1936 the MAVAG plant began to turn out guns and ammunition not only for Hungary but for other nations as well. The MAVAG plant produced parts for supply back to Sweden but orders were taken from Egypt, Finland, Holland, Lithuania, Norway and China. By 1939 even the United Kingdom placed orders but these, like most of the other export orders, were destined never to be fulfilled for the upheavals of 1939 put an end to such transactions. So the bulk of the MAVAG output went to the Hungarian forces for use as the 40 mm 36 M, and it seems very likely that some were passed on to the Germans.

Almost alone among the nations allied to Germany after 1941, Hungary enjoyed a great deal of

for military modellers

Hungarian artillery data

Field Guns	75 mm 15 M	75 mm 15/31 M	75 mm 15/35 M	8 cm 5/8 M	10.5 cm 37 M
Calibre	75 mm	75 mm	75 mm	80 mm	105 mm
Length of piece	1,155 mm	1,155 mm	1,155 mm	2,295 mm	2,941 mm
Weight in action	614 kg	770 kg	670 kg	1,065 kg	2,040 kg
Elevation	−10° to +50°	−10° to +50°	−10° to +50°	−7½° to +18°	−5° to +42°
Traverse	7°	7°	7°	8°	56°
MV	349 m/s	349 m/s	349 m/s	433 m/s	470 m/s
Shell weight	6.4 kg	6.4 kg	6.4 kg	6.4 kg	14.81 kg
Range	8,250 m	8,250 m	8,250 m	7,000 m	10,675 m

	30.5 cm 16 M	Anti-tank guns	37 mm 36 M	40 mm 40 M	47 mm 36 M
Calibre	305 mm	Calibre	37 mm	40 mm	47 mm
Length of piece	3,050 mm	Length of piece	1,665 mm	?	1,579 mm
Weight in action	20,880 kg	Weight in action	328 kg	430 kg	568 kg
Elevation	+40° to +75°	Elevation	−8° to +25°	−8° to +25°	−3° to +20°
Traverse	120°	Traverse	60°	58°	40°
MV	407 m/s	MV	762 m/s	824 m/s	720 m/s
Shell weight	287 kg	Shot weight	0.68 kg	0.965 kg	1.5 kg
Range	11,000 m	Effective range (max)	800 m	1,000 m	1,000 m

Below *40 mm 36 M. This picture is probably one of the first MAVAG versions produced as it is manned by civilians.* **Right** *20 mm 33 M seen here manned by Danish troops — the Hungarian version was virtually identical.* **Below right** *8 cm 29/38 M, another Bofors product.*

	10.5 cm 40 M	10.5 cm 31 M	15 cm 31 M	15 cm 14/35 M	15 cm 14/39 M	21 cm 40 M
Calibre	105 mm	105 mm	149.3 mm	149.1 mm	149.1 mm	210 mm
Length of piece	2,153 mm	5,250 mm	3,578 mm	2,088 mm*	2,088 mm*	5,000 mm
Weight in action	1,550 kg	6,000 kg	6,000 kg	2,965 kg	3,200 kg	15,022 kg
Elevation	−5° to +45°	−5° to +45°	−5° to +45°	−5° to +70°	−5° to +70°	0° to +70°
Traverse	8°	45°	45°	8°	8°	75°
MV	510 m/s	835 m/s	583 m/s	420 m/s	420 m/s	553 m/s
Shell weight	17.3 kg	17.5 kg	47 kg	42 kg	42 kg	102 kg
Effective ceiling	11,400 m	19,700 m	14,700 m	10,700 m	10,700 m	15,100 m

*approx

AA guns	50 mm 38 M	75 mm 40 M	20 mm 33 M	40 mm 36 M	80 mm 29/38 M
Calibre	50 mm	75 mm	20 mm	40 mm	80 mm
Length of piece	3,000 mm	3,450 mm	1,200 mm	2,400 mm	4,000 mm
Weight in action	1,000 kg	1,425 kg	260 kg	2,100 kg	3,100 kg
Elevation	−8° to +27°	−6° to +22°	−5° to +85°	−5° to +90°	−5° to +80°
Traverse	65°	65°	360°	360°	360°
MV	835 m/s	750 m/s	730 m/s	850 m/s	750 m/s
Shell weight	2.06 kg	4.1 kg	0.29 kg	0.965 kg	8 kg
Effective ceiling	1,500 m	1,800 m	2,120 m	9,400 m	9,700 m
Rate of fire(prac)			125 rpm	120 rpm	15 rpm

freedom and lack of interference in internal affairs. Doubtless, this was due to its food production and industrial capacity which supplied the Germans with much-needed agricultural and raw materials. Another factor was the military usefulness of the Hungarian forces. In 1939 Hungary had seven Army Corps, two cavalry brigades and two (incomplete) motorised brigades. The artillery park had 140 anti-tank guns and about 112 artillery pieces of all types, excluding anti-aircraft guns. By late 1940 the Army had expanded to 24 divisions and at the start of the Eastern Campaign, Hungary had some 30,000 men in the line. At the height of Hungarian involvement there were three motorised and one cavalry brigade fighting alongside the Germans, where on several occasions the cavalry performed many useful and heroic actions on the wide Russian Steppes.

But as stated above, on many occasions the Hungarian forces took some terrible beatings and as time went by the Hungarians lost much of their equipment and many of their best formations to the Soviet massed attacks of late 1942 and early 1943. By the winter of 1943-1944 the Hungarian war effort was virtually nil and by early 1944 the Hungarian government was attempting to put out peace feelers to the Western governments. Needless to say the Germans were able to detect these feelers on their extensive undercover network and the result was a German take-over of the Hungarian state in March 1944.

A great deal of research into the armies of Hungary, Rumania and Bulgaria still remains to be done, and this feature has only been able to skate the surface. Doubtless there are a large number of historians and enthusiastic amateurs like myself who are busy delving away into such matters but if there are, I have yet to hear from them. All I get is the North African campaign all over again . . . So if in any way this article has sparked off an interest all I can say is, pursue it. You will be amazed at the range of campaigns, battles and equipments, to say nothing of uniforms, which are as yet virtually unknown in the West. All it needs is a bit of effort. □

for military modellers

Napoleonic brigade tactics

Paddy Griffiths provides some stimulating food for thought for Napoleonic wargamers

While thinking about my existing Napoleonic wargames one day, I suddenly realised that there was a very serious gap in the types of actions which I could cover. Patrol and outpost action was all right, since skirmish games could be played. Army Corps battles were covered by the mainstream of 5, 15 and 25 mm rules. Whole armies could be manoeuvred on maps or in board games. At first sight the whole spectrum of Napoleonic tactics seemed to be covered — until I remembered the brigade.

In Wellington's army the brigade was usually composed of about three battalions with perhaps a company of rifles attached. Depending on the tactical needs of the moment there might be an artillery battery and even a squadron of cavalry. It was the lowest conceivable all-arms force. In continental armies the position was rather less clear-cut,

ranging from the Prussians' brigades of practically divisional strength, to the French ones, which sometimes became indistinguishable from their many-battalion regiments. The brigade was not, therefore, a standard unit. If two opposing brigades met, there could be an enormous number of interesting variations and imbalances built into the tactical problem.

This therefore seemed a good level to wargame. It had another advantage, too. This was that it came at precisely the tactical level where large unit combinations are recognisably influenced by the individual soldier. It is not totally personal, like platoon skirmishing, neither is it entirely high level 'grand tactics'. It is just between the two. The wargamer can really get down to the nitty-gritty of drill movements, volley firing and squad morale, without having to worry about a major battle strategy at the same time. He is no longer a Field Marshal, it is true; but by becoming a Colonel he can view the battle with a new and refreshing perspective.

This set me thinking. A number of readily available rule books (such as Bruce Quarrie's) certainly go into considerable detail about tactics inside the battalion — what each company can do, and so on — and it would be possible to play a brigade wargame simply using these rules. What I was looking for, however, was a set of rules which would be even more detailed still. They would have a basic playing unit even smaller than a company, and would analyse not just what the battalion commander told his companies to do, but also what the company commanders told their own sub-units to do. I therefore decided to have a go at a set of brigade rules of my own.

The first thing to decide, as in all sets of rules, was the scale. Looking at Napoleonic drill books gave me the idea that it would be nice to use the same unit of distance as was actually used at the time, ie, the *toise,* which is French for a fathom, or six feet. Using this basis it would be simpler to convert a Napoleonic drill book direct into wargame rules than if it were necessary to turn everything into some other (anachronistic) system of measurement. I therefore said that one *toise* would be

The French 900th March Regiment has sighted the enemy and is deploying from its line of march. Each battalion is in column of platoons, with skirmishers thrown out ahead and a battalion ammunition caisson near the rear of the column. There is also a cavalry squadron near the van.

Above *The left-hand battalion is deploying behind a hedge as the regimental command group makes its appreciation beneath the tree. The centre battalion is in process of taking its dressing after deploying into open column of divisions (each 'division' = a line of two companies). The right-hand battalion is wheeling into position to take up a similar formation. British cavalry has appeared on the right of the picture, and is about to engage the French cavalry, which is slightly disordered, as it has had to change front rather unexpectedly. Note some of the skirmishers have already opened involuntary fire.* **Below** *Rear view of the same: note that British artillery (one battery) is seen deployed and firing in the distance.*

---

represented in the game by 5 mm, or one yard would represent about 200 *toises*. For those who insist on being anachronistic, this works out at about one yard = 400 yards, or nine inches = 100 yards. Close musketry range is therefore five inches; long musket range is two feet; and long artillery range is around seven feet.

In order to ensure that the requisite detail could

be achieved, each move was set at the time needed to load and fire a field gun — 30 seconds. This meant that every shot could be plotted. Infantry would either load *or* fire in a turn. Only particularly fresh or well-trained troops could do both in the time, and no one would be allowed to fire on the move. In each turn the infantry would be allowed to march 25 *toises* in the open on good going, or 15

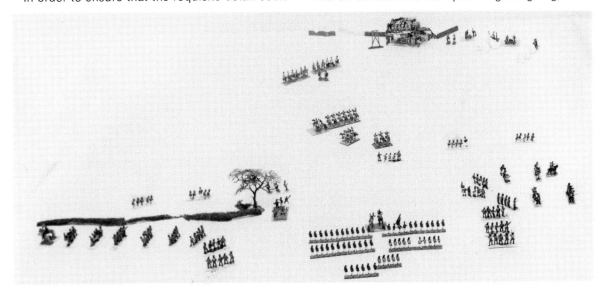

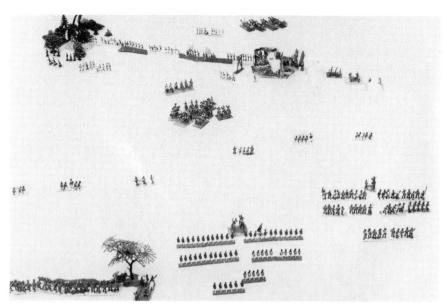

The cavalry is now engaged. The British, being more in hand, have launched only half a squadron, which has succeeded in involving the whole French squadron, and throwing it all into the confusion of the mêlée. The British cavalry therefore has a reserve still in hand. The French infantry has now fully formed its attack columns, while on the far side the British defensive line is seen, formed by 2/South Armagh Rangers, with a company of rifles in the wood on the left.

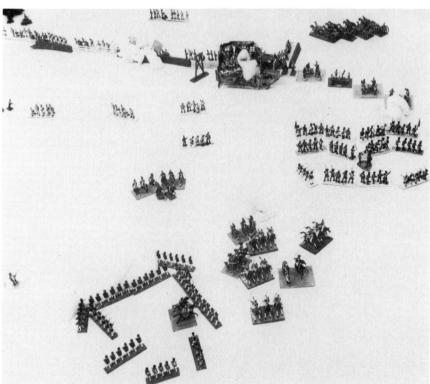

The British cavalry has now committed its formed reserve into the cavalry mêlée, driving it all off pell mell together, but itself stopping quickly, still in formation. The two French assault battalions are now in trouble: the right flank one has made a long approach under artillery fire, and is now stopped short under canister fire at close range. Notice the wavering in the ranks and spontaneous musketry fire. The central French battalion is rapidly trying to form square, but there is also some spontaneous musketry here, too. Nor is the British line totally free from the same problem: certain platoons have been tempted to try long-range shots too soon.

toises in bad going. Cavalry might vary from 25 to 50 *toises* per turn, depending on the going, the type of cavalry, and whether they were walking, trotting or galloping. An officer would be allowed to transmit one written or two verbal orders per turn. The speed of communication, in fact, becomes very important indeed in a game set at this level, as we shall see. A further complication is that to make an order which is not recognised in the drill book (eg, 'form a triangle against cavalry'!), an officer needs

three times the normal command time to make himself understood.

As for figure scale, I used our club's collection of Airfix 25 mm Napoleonics (along with many conversions from other Airfix sets), and found the best thing to do was to take each figure to represent ten men, and each model gun or vehicle to represent four.

Each battalion would need between 50 and 100 figures, depending on strength. As a rule of thumb it seems fair to take Napoleonic battalions as about 6-700 men, although it is easy enough to find historical examples which were far more or (more likely) far less. Our model battalions, at any rate, are already considerably bigger than is normal in wargames; but if we wish to make the individual platoon our basic unit this will be unavoidable. The best thing to do is to mount every five figures on to a card base to represent a platoon. In that way it will be easy to see which platoon is which, and they will also be easy to handle. The frontage of 'continental' platoon bases should be about two inches, with the figures placed upon them in a single line facing the front. This represents a platoon in line three deep with a fourth line or *serre-file* for the officers and NCOs. In the case of 'British' units the base should be 2½ inches long, representing a platoon in two-deep line, plus a third line of officers and NCOs. It will be found that for all drill movements these are the fundamental formations. A column of platoons, for example, was standard for marching up a road. The only exception, if it could be called such, is when the platoon moves to its flank (ie, moves 'sideways' in column of threes). In that case the figures will be facing the wrong way on their bases, although the shape of the bases themselves will still be correct.

As for cavalry and artillery, a cavalry squadron would be represented by about 12 figures, which would be split down into four section units, each of three figures on a base. An artillery battery would consist of three or four model cannon, and three or four model caissons, each stuck on to a base with two or three gunner figures. Thus the battery would be split into gun sections (each representing two guns plus their limbers of ready-use ammunition and teams), and ammunition sections (each representing four reserve caissons). The total number of vehicles represented would therefore come to about 30, which is historically about right for a Napoleonic battery.

Each infantry battalion, cavalry squadron and artillery battery would, in addition, have a small command group on a base. This would represent the unit commander, his second in command, any other hangers-on who might be around, as well as (for game purposes) a limitless number of runners to take messages. In addition each brigade would have a rather larger tray of staff officers to represent brigade HQ. If desired, there could also be a brigade wagon train for supplies, although in most tactical circumstances this would be left well to the rear.

A point to notice at this stage is that the figures need not be made detachable from their bases, as casualties are not scored in terms of individual figures, but in 'status points'. Each platoon or section has a reference number and a status value. The players keep a list of their platoons' reference numbers, and record the loss of status against each one as it happens. This represents killed, wounded, and, most important of all, morale. When a unit is

Close-up of the completed square, repelling the British half squadron. Note the grenadier platoons at the angles of the square.

reduced to status 'F' it is removed from the game. A guard or veteran unit (eg, the flank companies of a line battalion) will have an initial status of 'A'. A reasonable line unit will start at 'B', and a raw conscript or reserve unit will start at 'C'. After receiving fire or running away from attacks each unit may lose status until it gets down to 'F', which is the breaking point. This is when all the soldiers left in the line make mumbled excuses and evaporate to the rear.

Having established our opposing brigades, and decided the initial status of each platoon, we are ready to start the game. A point to note is that buildings will be nearer a 'one-to-one' scale than in most wargames. Instead of holding a whole battalion, they should only take about a company each, unless they are particularly large.

It is not my intention to give the rules in full, as space does not allow it. Many of the underlying concepts will, in any case, already be familiar to wargamers. I will therefore concentrate on the points which seem to be most different from normal wargames. First of all, laying out the initial dispositions.

A very great deal depends upon this phase of the operation, because the formation in which each battalion is originally deployed may turn out to be crucial later on. A feature of this game is the cumbersome difficulty of performing any tactical evolution, particularly under fire. It was a maxim of many Napoleonic soldiers that 'any unit which manoeuvres (ie, *tries formation changes,* etc) near the enemy is in a state of crisis'. Not only must each soldier *move* the full distance required (eg, a flank company deploying into column at the far end of

The French battalion before the guns is starting to break up and is milling round in confusion. It is not allowed to advance, under the morale rules, but cannot yet retreat, as the orders have not yet been passed down.

The British cavalry is retiring to re-form, the French right assault battalion is at last pulling back, while the French commander has ordered the central battalion to cover the move by deploying into line. He has also ordered forward his left, reserve battalion, which is now making rather a meal of crossing the hedge; some of its platoons have decided they would prefer to fire at enemy skirmishers, who have crept up to range now.

The central French battalion has now fully deployed, but the hedge-crossing unit still has as many difficulties as before, and is suffering from accurate rifle fire.

Close-up of the battalion attempting to cross the hedge, showing how it is divided between formed companies and platoons which are still firing wildly.

the battalion line might have to move for three whole turns), but time must also be allowed for the movement to be ordered by the battalion commander, and then relayed by each company commander in turn. Finally, when the formation change is complete, the whole battalion must spend a move recovering its dressing, since the act of changing formation is considered to have created a certain disorder in the ranks. The same is true of crossing obstacles or opening fire. Anything which might cause an upset to the precision of the drill will require a 'dressing' turn to correct. Otherwise that battalion will have to fight with greatly reduced cohesion.

Voice range is only 15 *toises,* so it will be impossible to issue one order which everyone will hear. Some form of relay will be needed, which will help make any change of plans a frighteningly lengthy affair. Advantages will therefore be gained by a player who has the foresight to put his troops into appropriate formations well in advance. He will save risky reorganisations at moments when he is vulnerable to attack.

A major bane of Napoleonic tacticians' lives was the fact that troops often opened fire before they were ordered. The Spanish at Talavera even opened a sustained fire while the enemy were still a kilometre distant. In our game, therefore, we test morale as soon as the enemy comes into sight. A percentage die is thrown, and each platoon which scores a '0' will at once open a panic fire. This may be stopped on subsequent turns for anything between a 4 and a 9, but that platoon will still need to be dressed back into order. If its fire continues more than one turn, then its neighbouring platoons will have to throw to see if they are affected by the rot, and so on. In this way a spontaneous fire may spread down the whole line. With low grade troops

the dice score to stop the spread will be harder to achieve than with well trained ones.

Both sides again test for spontaneous opening of fire whenever a target is presented within 100 *toises* of each platoon. 'A' grade open for 0 or 1; 'B' grade for 0, 1 or 2; and 'C' grade for 0, 1, 2 or 3. Note that this applies only to front rank troops who have loaded muskets. It was quite common for Napoleonic officers to send troops forward unloaded, in the hope that they would not stop to fire. Only too often in attacks troops who did stop to fire would be impossible to urge forward for the final assault. In our rules, therefore, it should be difficult to persuade any troops to stop firing once

Close-up of the retreat of the French right-hand battalion, leaving behind as skirmishers those troops which are completely out of control.

for military modellers

they have started, and even more difficult to advance again afterwards.

Without going into details, the effects of fire are relatively easy to assess. A firing platoon which throws a '9' on one die at long range, or 5, 6, 7, 8 or 9 at close range, will reduce one enemy platoon by one status grade. This basic rule, obviously, has to be adjusted to suit variables such as targets behind cover, or firing units using their first, carefully loaded, volley. Skirmishers, also, will always score about double the hits to be expected from units in line.

When units have come to close musket range, the defenders must test morale if the other side wishes to continue his advance with the bayonet. Relative strength and status are involved in this dice throw, as well as relative positions (uphill, downhill, cover, disorganisation, etc). In essence, however, this rule is rather similar to many which are already in use in the wargaming world, so I do not intend to reproduce it here in full. Suffice to say that the two opposing units will have reached one of two possible results before bayonets are actually crossed. Either the defender will have run away because his morale dice were not high enough to allow him to stand; or the attacker will have come to a halt because the defender's dice *did* allow him to stand firm. In the latter case the defender is then free to start the procedure for mounting a counter-attack, or volley firing, if he wishes. The original attacker will in this case be unable to reply effectively, since he will still be shaken from his failed assault.

The rules for cavalry are basically similar to those for infantry, although it is less likely that the cavalry will open fire at long range. (It is still possible; there were many cases of this happening in the Napoleonic wars.) When they come into a charge, however, they have a choice of speeds. The faster they go, the more they have individual impetus, but the less they have unit cohesion. At 100 *toises* from the enemy individual sections may spontaneously lose cohesion and accelerate before their commanders order it, in which case a lot of the power of their attack will be lost. The chances of this happening are higher if dressing has been lost, or if the commanders were trying to advance at the trot or gallop in the first place. At the walk, on the other hand, commanders have less chance of losing their men in a wild rush, and more chance of arriving on the target in a compact body. In any case it will be very difficult for cavalry to overrun formed infantry which is not disorganised, unless it strikes at an open flank.

As for artillery, it takes two turns to unlimber horse and heavy guns, and one to unlimber medium foot pieces. If the guns are then to be moved, they can either be limbered up again, or

General view as the French left-hand battalion has finally cleared the hedge and at last formed into assault column of divisions. In subsequent moves the British artillery had to re-stock with ammunition from its caissons, as it had fired the ten shots from its ready chests. The British infantry held its position and repulsed the ill co-ordinated attacks first of the French left flank battalion, then of the French centre battalion, both of which had been considerably softened by preliminary artillery and skirmisher fire. The lesson of this action was that it is much easier to control troops who are standing still behind cover than it is to conduct complicated manoeuvres, especially under fire. The Napoleonic battalion is a much more unwieldly creature than is often assumed.

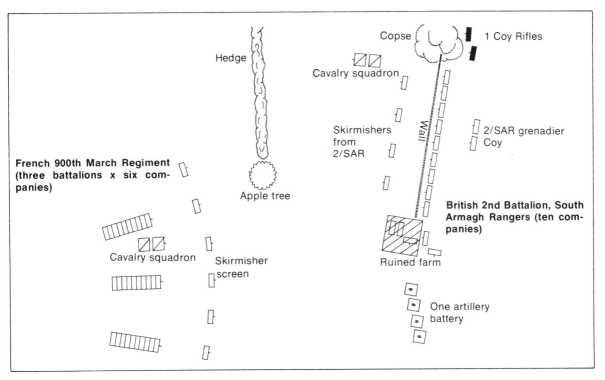

Copse

1 Coy Rifles

Cavalry squadron

Hedge

Wall

2/SAR grenadier Coy

Skirmishers from 2/SAR

French 900th March Regiment (three battalions x six companies)

Apple tree

British 2nd Battalion, South Armagh Rangers (ten companies)

Cavalry squadron

Skirmisher screen

Ruined farm

One artillery battery

manhandled at quarter speed on drag ropes. If fire is to be applied to a flank of the battery position it will obviously be important to manoeuvre the guns into sites where they do not interfere with each other's field of fire. Another aspect of the battery siting problem is that the reserve ammunition must be put in a covered position where it is near enough to replenish the guns, but safe from enemy fire. The guns themselves are deemed to carry only ten rounds each, in their immediate limbers, so the arrangements for re-supply may have an important influence on tactics.

Gunners are considered to be able to hold their fire until they receive an order; although when the enemy comes to short musket range they must throw dice to see if they desert their pieces. At long range each section of guns will hit if a 9 is thrown on one die. This reduces an enemy by one status point per platoon in a direct line for 50 *toises* directly behind the point of aim (further if ricochet fire is used). Thus fire against columns can be very damaging, while fire against well spaced lines will be relatively light. At canister range casualties are taken off the target's first rank platoons only, but one status point is removed from each for a 5 or 6; two points for a 7 or 8; and three points for a 9. Obviously these scores are adjusted if the gunners are shaken, if the guns are heavier or lighter than normal, or if the target has cover.

There are many further points which could be made about the brigade game, but I hope that there is already enough here to give an idea of the sort of battles which it produces. There seem to be two major differences between this game and the nor-

mal ones set at divisional or army Corps level. Firstly, the units are bigger, and therefore the player must pay much more attention to passing orders, anticipating developments, and choosing the correct drills. In one of our games a player spent three moves just trying to decide which of four different drill methods he should use to get a single battalion from column into line. The result was confusion. The units seem so huge and unwieldy on the table that they have navigation problems rather like those heavy oil tankers which do not respond to the rudder until they are two miles further on. This is bad enough, but it also means that the risks of traffic jams are greatly increased. This game therefore cures the wargamer of any tendency he may have had to think of a battalion as a nippy little 20-man affair.

The second difference between this game and many others is that it allows the battle to be seen in personal terms very similar to those of a skirmish wargame. The morale of each platoon makes a difference. All sorts of infuriating things can happen, such as the premature opening of fire, or the involuntary splitting of a battalion as one half becomes snared in an obstacle while the other is marching blithely ahead, obeying outdated orders. Individual platoons seem to take on minds of their own; they are certainly no longer mere pawns which obey orders automatically and instantly. In this type of wargame the player starts to realise that the biggest problem in war is persuading your own men to do the right thing. Compared with that, the business of actually fighting the enemy seems relatively simple. □

THE BIG ONE

Gerald Scarborough shows how to model the famous Mack NO in 1:76 scale

'Made-to-order for the world's toughest customer . . . The Army's newest and biggest Prime Mover is probably the best single job in truck history. Most of its details can't be made public . . . but you can see for yourself that it's BIG. And we can tell you that it hooks up to a whale of a big gun, takes on a terrific load and goes almost anywhere except straight up'.

And that is how part of the Mack advert ran in the *Saturday Evening Post* in November 1942. The 'whale of a big gun' was the 155 mm Long Tom or alternatively the 8-inch Howitzer and the Mack NO was used basically as a Prime Mover for this heavy artillery but also as a cargo and personnel carrier.

Without doubt it was strongly built with a gross

Title photo *Head-on view of the impressive Mack NO still in civilian use in the 1970s. Only the side lights, indicators and mirrors are clues that it is not on military service.*

weight of 43,570 lb, could carry a payload of 15,450 lb, had a maximum drawbar pull of 43,200 lb, though the normal towed load was 32,000 lb and had a winch capacity of 40,000 lb.

The six-cylinder in-line, 707 cubic inch (11,585 cc), 156 net hp engine ran on 70 octane petrol and the vehicle carried 160 gallons of fuel. Maximum grade capability was 65 per cent while maximum road speed was about 32 mph with towed load. Power to the three axles was via a five-speed and reverse gearbox and a two-speed transfer case divided power between front and rear axles. The drive to the front axle could be disengaged if required. To stop the vehicle air brakes with a hand-controlled air line to the trailer brakes and a disc parking brake were fitted.

Below *This front three-quarter shot emphasises the bulk of this prime mover. The hoist is an unfortunate civilian modification.* **Below right** *Rear three-quarter view shows the stubs of the original trail hoist frame still inside the body.*

Above *Nearside front wheel detail, also fuel tank with what is not an original frame on the side.* **Above right** *Detail of the front axle shows offset differential, springs, shock absorbers and spring hanger brackets. Note also the large rectangular sump and bearing bracket for the winch.* **Right** *The winch barrel is below the upswept centre of the bumper. Also visible is the front hub and steering linkage.* **Below right** *The rear wheels are ten stud fixing and are well dished.*

Of particular interest was the drive to the front axle which dispensed with the usual universal joints by employing the king pin shafts as intermediate drive shafts. The drive from the differential went through half shafts to bevel gears on the king pins which were in bearings on the axle casting and then through a second set of bevels to the hubs. This permitted a high axle ground clearance and allowed the necessary reduction ratios between differential and hub. The rear axles incorporated planetary reductions in the hubs.

The body of the US Army Standard cargo type was an open-type cab with removable top and windscreen. A section of the slatted sides folded down to form bench seats and spare wheel stowage was arranged at the front of each side. A tubular hoop at the rear was fitted with a chain hoist for lifting the gun trail on to the sprung pintle hook and clamp.

There are still a few of these vehicles to be found in civilian use and it was such a vehicle that I was able to photograph. It differed very slightly from the military type and basically only the hoist hoop had been cut off and a hydraulic hoist frame had been fitted. Minor alterations to adapt the lighting to current regulations had also been made.

Nevertheless I think the detail shown will be of value to the scratch-builder and the following few notes may be helpful as suggested construction ideas for a model in 1:76 scale. Of course a little compromise may have to be accepted as there are no exact style wheels or axles, for example, that we can use from kits so far on the market. Fortunately the Airfix vehicle range is extensive and the choice boils down to what you have available in your spares box. I would take the Scammell tank trans-

for military modellers

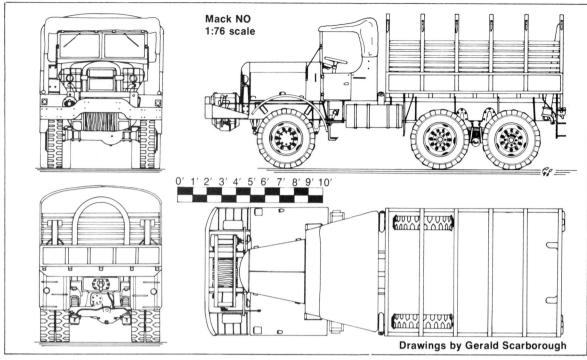

Mack NO
1:76 scale

0' 1' 2' 3' 4' 5' 6' 7' 8' 9' 10'

Drawings by Gerald Scarborough

Below Note the towing hook on the end of the chassis and the brackets, into which the tubular hoist frame fits, which are shown each side of the chassis frame. Towing eyes would fit in the holes under these brackets. Note the spring ends fit into the boxes under the axles. **Bottom** The massive bracket which supports the rear spring and is bolted to the main chassis frame. **Right** A hodge-podge ot new lights, indicators and reflectors mar the near mudguard but the original access steps and reflectors are still visible.

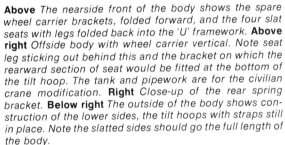

Above *The nearside front of the body shows the spare wheel carrier brackets, folded forward, and the four slat seats with legs folded back into the 'U' framework.* **Above right** *Offside body with wheel carrier vertical. Note seat leg sticking out behind this and the bracket on which the rearward section of seat would be fitted at the bottom of the tilt hoop. The tank and pipework are for the civilian crane modification.* **Right** *Close-up of the rear spring bracket.* **Below right** *The outside of the body shows construction of the lower sides, the tilt hoops with straps still in place. Note the slatted sides should go the full length of the body.*

porter trailer wheels as first choice with the AEC Matador refueller as second or even a combination of both. Additional wheels could come from the Airfix Recovery Set and those on the back of the Thornycroft crane are similar to the tank transporter.

All the wheels have to be thinned down slightly for the eight rear wheels and this is easiest to do with the tank transporter wheels as they can be thinned by filing the inside faces of the two halves of each wheel. The centres of the outside four are fitted with a punched plastic card disc and a short length of round sprue to represent the hub centre. A refinement is to drill out the centre of the outside four wheels to accentuate the 'dish' and to replace with a plastic card disc insert impressed with wheel nut detail from the inside. The front wheels are similar but use these with the non-detailed side to the outside and fit with a centre from the Matchbox M3 half track with the central projecting hub removed. The alternative is to build up the centre and detail with 'nuts' cut from plastic rod.

for military modellers

Above *The single driver's seat and the two-passenger bench seat. There is no truth in the rumour that it took three men to haul on the steering — two were quite sufficient.* **Above right** *Straight through the cab gives view of the pedals and levers. Note inside far door handle and data plates on door, also small instrument panel on the steering column mounting bracket.* **Below** *The six-cylinder engine amply fills the massive bonnet space.* **Below right** *This view of the engine shows the fan and its drive belts with the hose connections to the radiator. Note the brackets at the rear of the bonnet in which the windscreen supports slide.*

The next requirement is suitable axles and these present a problem in that the differential housings are not central. The front axle from the Airfix AEC Refueller can be used for the front of the Mack and if you have another spare it could be used as the rear of the pair of back axles. Note the inside of the front wheels should have the centre hole filled and a fresh hole drilled to locate the axle above the centre line. The photographs should provide sufficient information for detailing with brackets, 'U' bolts, trackrod, and shock absorbers, etc.

Above *Detail of winch drive from the offside.* **Above right** *The headlamps are mounted on brackets from the chassis side frames and protected by wire mesh guards. Note winch control rod and linkage.*

The rear axles are similarly adapted with the addition of the overhead drive shaft, on top and alongside the top of the differential housing, the air brake cylinders, and pipe work.

The chassis can be constructed from Plastruct channel section or alternatively from strips cut from 60 thou plastic card sheet. Allow for plenty of intermediate cross-members and make absolutely certain it does not warp while the cement joints are setting. The axle mounting brackets are made from scrap and these should be attached to the underside of the chassis frame and springs, either from the spares box, or built up with Microstrip cemented in place. Again the detail photographs will help here as they show up parts which cannot be included in the drawings. A dummy engine sump should be cemented in place or you may be able to make up a dummy engine as one side of this is shown on a photograph. Unfortunately I could not raise the bonnet on the other side to get at the detail there.

The next stage is the rear body which can be treated as a sub-assembly to be cemented to the chassis when completed or with the bonnet/cab section. Note that the lower body sides on the vehicle photographed appear to have been modified from the originals which were not 'boxed in' but are as shown in the drawings and in the photographs of the front part of the offside.

The lower four of the six slats are designed to fold down to form seats, the legs of which fold into the channel sections to which the slats are bolted. Note the first two sections fold down separately to the three rear sections. The body should be based on a 30 or 40 thou plastic card floor underneath which are the transverse body bearers which in turn are mounted on longitudinal chassis runners. All these can be cut and shaped from plastic card to the underside of the floor. Above the floor build up

the lower sides detailed with thick Microstrip on the outside. Drill the floor to take the tubular chain hoist frame at the rear which goes through into brackets on the main chassis frame. Inside the body two spare wheel carriers are mounted along the sides at the front. A hinged tail door is fitted at the rear.

The cab and bonnet section are constructed to a common floor to which these are built up as the drawings. A driver's seat and a two-passenger bench seat are fitted inside and the interior views show the layout of controls and dashboard. Twin rectangular fuel tanks are fitted below the cab/body with long filler necks between. Note the access steps under the cab, the lower section of which is hinged to fold up. An air cylinder for the braking system is housed under the cab on the offside. The massive winch is bolted to the front of the chassis and the framework for this is built up from Microstrip, plastic card and Plastruct angle which is useful for the cross mountings. The winch can be

Close-up of winch brackets and control rods, also POW carrier.

Above *Step detail and brake air cylinder on the offside.*
Above right *The end.*

controlled from the cab and the actuating rods are clearly shown in the photographs.

The front mudguards are moulded from plastic strip as usual by wrapping round wooden dowel, holding in place with masking tape and immersing in boiling water for a few seconds then in cold water to set the shape. The massive front bumper is built up from 40 thou plastic card with the step grids from plastic rod. Note the Petrol/Oil/Water container holders each side. There is some interest-

ing and intricate modelling to detail the front end all of which should be visible on the photographs to back up the basic drawings. Note that the large round lights on top of the front mudguards are flashing indicator lights, a later addition. The original side lights were slightly forward of these. On the original vehicle a circular reflector was fitted on the wedge-shaped box on the mudguard front.

Although it is in 1:72 scale there is a kit of the 155 mm Long Tom gun by Hasegawa and notwithstanding the difference in scales this does make an impressive train to add to any collection of World War 2 military equipment. ☐

MODELLING THE WAR WITH JAPAN

Bryan Perrett with some scenario ideas for dioramas with an Oriental flavour

'These men wore turbans and steel helmets and slouch hats, and berets and tank helmets, and khaki shakos inherited from the eighteenth century.' So wrote John Masters in the memorable description of 14th Army contained in the second volume of his autobiography *The Road Past Mandalay;* and many of these men have fortunately been reproduced by Airfix in their 00/HO range of figures, plus, of course, Japanese and American troops, providing the diorama maker with first-rate raw material which, with a little work, can be converted to provide a wide variety of types.

For example, the Gurkhas, minus kukri, will pass as Thais, who fought alongside the Japanese during the 1942 fighting in the Philippines and elsewhere American troops were still wearing British-pattern steel helmets; the Australian set can do duty either as themselves, or as British infantry in Burma; the British infantry set, suitably painted, can act as Indian infantry, although it should be remembered that if one wishes to represent a Sikh battalion or tank squadron, turbans are the inflexible rule. Other troops, such as the Frontier Force Rifles and the Chinese,

wore a floppy peaked cap, which some careful carving on an American Civil War Federal infantry head can reproduce.

Personally, I consider 1:76 to be the ideal scale for dioramic reproduction of incidents in this theatre of war, as much of the fighting took place at close range and there is little difficulty in bringing the enemy into the picture. There is no reason at all why 1:32 scale models should not produce an interesting representation of a local situation, and indeed the new Airfix Lee provides an ideal starting

---

Below left *Incident in the Ngakyedauk Pass. A skeleton diorama using basic sand table material and largely unpainted subjects. All figures except vehicle crews are un-modified 1:76 Airfix from the inexpensive boxed sets. Equipment includes an Airfix 5.5-inch howitzer from the Matador and gun set, one Airfix and one Hasegawa Lee. The Hasegawa model has a messy 37 mm mounting, but the running gear assembly is slightly simpler than that of Airfix model.* **Below** *Badan Singh and the Type 97. Another skeleton diorama described in the text, featuring an Airfix Type 97 and a Hasegawa Humber armoured car. The Airfix jungle outpost kit provides a background.*

Above *Difficulties of village fighting in Burma. The earth banks surrounding each dwelling often proved to be a tank obstacle. In this case the Japanese are mounting a desperate counter-attack on the infantry escort. Again, the Airfix jungle outpost set provides a good setting.*
Above right *116 Regiment RAC's first attack on the Springs. As described in the text of the article, the diorama shows the climax of the action, when the Japanese suffered severely trying to deal with the troop in the defile. The Shermans are all Airfix.*

point, but if it is intended to depict a particular event, then real depth and breadth can only be achieved at the smaller scale.

There is also plenty of hardware available throughout the market in this scale, and little difficulty should be experienced in obtaining most AFV requirements. The Japanese used the Type 94 tankette, the Type 95 light tank, and the medium Type 97, which was their mainstay, although an older medium, the Type 89, was still in service in 1942, and latterly a number of self-propelled guns, based on the Type 97 chassis, also saw service. On the Allied side, Stuarts were used throughout the war in Burma, in the Philippines, the Pacific, and by the Australians in New Guinea; Lees were used extensively in Burma; Shermans were employed in the closing stages in Burma, during the reconquest of the Philippines, and in other island landings; the Matilda was popular with the Australians in New Guinea, on Bougainville, Labuan and Balikpapan; the New Zealand Army employed a squadron of Valentines in the Solomon Islands, and more Valentines were used in Burma, primarily the scissors-bridge version, although a handful of gun tanks saw action in 1943. A regiment of M7 self-propelled guns took part in the fighting along the Irrawaddy Bend and formed part of the advance guard during the advance on Rangoon, and more M7s and M8s

fought in the Philippines, as did M18 tank destroyers, while during the many island-hopping operations LVTs provided immediate fire support for the landing force.

There is, therefore, no shortage of subject matter, and perhaps the following anecdotes, chosen at random, will show that there is no shortage of suitable dramatic situations either.

. During the Arakan campaign of 1944 the headquarters of 7th Indian Division was besieged in an area known as the Admin Box. The Japanese were held at bay largely by the presence of 25th Dragoons' Lees within the box, but now and again they did secure a lodgement, and on one occasion butchered the patients and medical staff in the main dressing station.

Meanwhile, 5th Indian Division was pushing a relief column through the Ngakyedauk Pass, headed by a squadron composed of the Dragoons' spare tanks. Near the head of the pass the column was stalled by a large complex of bunkers. The Japanese were, of course, expert in bunker construction, and often only constant direct fire from tanks at close range could silence them, since conventional shelling and air attack seemed to make no impression. On this occasion, however, even the 75 mm guns of the Lees could not solve the problem, and after consultation with the division's CRA it was decided to resort to unconventional measures. A 5.5-inch howitzer was brought up, and with two Lees acting as a shield for the gunners, it proceeded to turn each bunker slit into a smoking crater. It was a most unusual role for medium artillery, but it broke the enemy's resistance, and allowed the relief column to fulfil its mission.

Two armoured car regiments saw service in Burma during the 1945 operations, 11th (Prince Albert Victor's Own) Light Cavalry, with Daimlers, and 16th Light Cavalry, with various marks of

Humber. All armoured car operations produce short, sharp little actions which can be reproduced in diorama form quite easily. Dafadar (Sergeant) Badan Singh's action outside Yamethin on April 10 1945 is a case in point.

Badan Singh had been patrolling towards the town from the north-west, and had paused to engage some dug-in infantry when a Type 97 medium tank barged out of cover 200 yards to his flank, and opened fire. The Japanese gunner missed by a whisker. Traversing smartly, Badan opened up with his 37 mm, which was already loaded with an HE shell. This burst on the enemy tank, and the next round, which was armour-piercing, penetrated and caused an explosion. As the Japanese crew scrambled out, Badan engaged with his machine-gun, killing them and some infantry who had accompanied the tank. Why the Type 97 commander chose to leave cover when he had the Humber cold is a mystery, but was entirely in keeping with the volatile nature of Japanese tank crew. For his skill and courage in defeating his larger opponent Badan Singh was awarded the Military Medal.

A battle of a different kind took place some two months earlier in the Philippines, at a small town called Munoz. Here the Japanese armour made a self-sacrificial stand which enabled many of their comrades to escape into the mountains, although it was not a tank battle in the conventional sense.

The Japanese armour, which consisted mostly of Type 97s, was dug in up to its turrets, with the tanks acting as strongpoints. They were difficult to spot, and provided a heavy volume of fire which kept the American infantry pinned down. Heavy artillery strikes destroyed a number of the dug-in tanks, but these were replaced at night. A counter attack led by tanks came to grief very quickly, but it took a week's hard fighting before the town was taken.

Above left *Ambush on Luzon. Using a dug-in Ho-Ni tank destroyer, the Japanese have caught the American advance guard in a classic 'L' ambush, but have sprung their trap a little early. A general view of the engagement, showing the Japanese position at the top and in the trees to the right of the track.* **Above** *The Ho-Ni, a neat Fujimi kit, has just scored a kill on the leading Sherman.*

The surviving Japanese tanks tried to break out to the north, only to find the Shermans of Company G, 44th Tank Battalion, waiting for them, and none got through.

The Japanese were never shy of Allied armour, and would willingly attack individual tanks with pole and satchel charges, or even swords, regardless of the chances of survival. In Burma 14th Army trained special units to act as a close infantry escort to the tanks, a vital provision in those parts of the country which afforded ample cover for potential attackers. These close escort duties were generally carried out by Bombay Grenadiers, a regiment for which tank crewmen who fought in Burma have only the highest praise. Perhaps one of the coolest actions performed by tank crew and Grenadiers together took place near Legyaing on March 27 1945.

A and C Squadrons, 116 Regiment RAC (Gordon Highlanders), were approaching the village when all hell suddenly broke, much of the defenders' fire coming from very close range. At this critical moment Corporal Morrison's tank coughed to a standstill with a petrol stoppage. Disregarding heavy rifle and automatic fire, Morrison clambered out and killed three Japanese soldiers in a bunker, using his Sten and grenades, and then organised his Grenadier escort and some Punjabi infantry into a covering party while he and his crew cleared the stoppage. He was also awarded the Military Medal.

A month earlier A Squadron had been involved in

Top *Using the knocked out Sherman for cover, an American bazooka team has doubled forward on the left flank and is preparing for a shot at the enemy tank destroyer.* **Above** *Casualties litter the ground behind the leading Sherman as the Americans head for cover. The second Sherman gives covering fire, but seems to be off target and could well be the Ho-Ni's second victim unless the commander orders reverse hard-right. In the lee of the tank the infantry platoon radio operator sends a contact report back to company.* **Below** *The Americans counter attack. The platoon leader (centre, firing pistol near tree) has correctly decided on a right flank attack which will roll up the Japanese 'L'. The men are shown moving into position. The remaining Sherman appears to have survived, and the situation looks as though it is back in hand. The Japanese will almost certainly lose their tank destroyer once the infantry support has been eliminated. American infantry taken from the Airfix US Marine set.*

a series of attacks on a location known as the Springs, near Letse, under the command of 28th East African Brigade. The Springs provides an excellent setting for a larger diorama, and consists of a ridge through the centre of which a dusty track follows a defile.

The Japanese opened fire on the advancing Shermans with mortars and machine-guns, and the squadron leader, Major Moir, directed one of his troops to circle round to the rear of the ridge. The Japanese swarmed out of their foxholes to deal with this threat, and suffered severely in the process from the guns of the remainder of the squadron.

Behind the ridge, the troop leader took a wrong turning and his tanks suddenly appeared again, coming through the defile. Meanwhile the squadron was climbing the ridge, and had crossed the crest when the Japanese launched a frenzied counter attack. They swarmed all over the tanks, in spite of the fire coming from the King's African Rifles, and one managed to get his grenade into a Sherman turret, starting a fire and wounding the commander and operator. The vehicle smashed into a tree, and although the gunner was shot dead while climbing out, the driver fought off the Japanese with his revolver while the wounded were carried away. Elsewhere the crew of a bogged down tank were forced to fight at close quarters until their vehicle could be towed out. Then, suddenly, the Japanese had gone.

The Springs attack had been mounted as part of the deception plan for 4 Corps' crossing of the Irrawaddy, and the area, once taken, was evacuated and re-occupied by the enemy. To focus their attention on it, it was attacked twice more by A Squadron and the East Africans, and taken each time. On the second occasion the enemy employed dug-in anti-tank guns at close range, which failed to penetrate the Shermans, although two tanks were disabled by mortar shells bursting on the engine decks. These were towed in later. The final attack was not as dramatic, as the enemy did not wait for the tanks to complete their assault, although they did mount a counter-raid of their own on A Squadron's harbour area, which was not a success.

These, then, are a few simple ideas for the construction of inexpensive dioramas portraying incidents which took place in a theatre of war which, until now, has been something of a Cinderella amongst military modellers. Research will reveal many more suitable incidents, and, fortunately, manufacturers seem to be producing more and more kits which have a bearing on a really vast and absorbing subject. For more information on armoured operations in the Far East, my recent book *Tank Tracks to Rangoon* (Robert Hale Ltd) may be found useful. ☐